Group Therapy for Adult Survivors of Childhood Abuse

This book presents the therapist with a reflective and robust framework for group treatment that promotes an end to the shame and secrecy so frequently experienced by survivors.

Through a series of tools such as visualisations and art exercises, the practitioner is guided through the process of establishing and running a group in this modality. The synthesis of both an educational and a process-based model is imbued with a sense of warmth and a deep understanding of this client group. Themes such as self-soothing, strengthening boundaries, inner-child work, making meaning of endings, and ways forward drive this therapeutic approach. Taking group work as the optimum matrix for change for this client population, this model provides a convincing rationale for the establishment of said work as best practice in the institutions that provide for their care.

Practicing therapists and mental health nurses will find this new model of therapy an instrumental resource in their approach to treatment for survivors of trauma and abuse.

Lorraine McColgan has a Masters in Counselling Psychology and a Diploma in Clinical Supervision from Trinity College Dublin. She works with the National Counselling Service in Ireland and in private practice as an individual and group therapist and as a clinical supervisor. She is a registered member of the Psychological Society of Ireland. Please contact lormccol@yahoo.co.uk for all inquiries.

"McColgan offers a practical guide to therapeutic group work for mental health professionals who work with adult survivors of abuse. Her therapeutic group work synthesises a psychoeducational approach with a dynamic process perspective ... I like this work. It is simple but profound. Unpretentious and eminently usable."

Jarlath F. Benson, *Psychoanalytic Group Analyst,*
Trainer and Supervisor with the NHS, UK
and in private practice, Ireland

Group Therapy for Adult Survivors of Childhood Abuse

A Practical Guide for Mental Health Professionals

Lorraine McColgan

LONDON AND NEW YORK

Cover image: Veleri / Getty images

First published 2022
by Routledge
4 Park Square, Milton Park, Abingdon, Oxon OX14 4RN

and by Routledge
605 Third Avenue, New York, NY 10158

Routledge is an imprint of the Taylor & Francis Group, an informa business

© 2022 Lorraine McColgan

The right of Lorraine McColgan to be identified as author of this work has been asserted in accordance with sections 77 and 78 of the Copyright, Designs and Patents Act 1988.

All rights reserved. No part of this book may be reprinted or reproduced or utilised in any form or by any electronic, mechanical, or other means, now known or hereafter invented, including photocopying and recording, or in any information storage or retrieval system, without permission in writing from the publishers.

Trademark notice: Product or corporate names may be trademarks or registered trademarks, and are used only for identification and explanation without intent to infringe.

British Library Cataloguing-in-Publication Data
A catalogue record for this book is available from the British Library

Library of Congress Cataloging-in-Publication Data
Names: McColgan, Lorraine, 1970– author.
Title: Group therapy for adult survivors of childhood abuse :
    a practical guide for mental health professionals / Lorraine
    McColgan.
Description: 1 Edition. | New York, NY : Routledge, 2022. |
    Includes bibliographical references and index. |
Identifiers: LCCN 2021045872 (print) | LCCN 2021045873 (ebook) |
    ISBN 9780367862565 (paperback) | ISBN 9781032215402 (hardback) |
    ISBN 9781003268888 (ebook)
Subjects: LCSH: Adult child abuse victims—Psychology. | Adult
    child abuse victims—Mental health. | Adult child abuse victims—
    Rehabilitation. | Group psychotherapy.
Classification: LCC HV6626.5 .M3883 2022 (print) | LCC HV6626.5 (ebook) |
    DDC 362.76/7—dc23/eng/20211109
LC record available at https://lccn.loc.gov/2021045872
LC ebook record available at https://lccn.loc.gov/2021045873

ISBN: 978-1-032-21540-2 (hbk)
ISBN: 978-0-367-86256-5 (pbk)
ISBN: 978-1-003-26888-8 (ebk)

DOI: 10.4324/9781003268888

Typeset in Times New Roman
by Apex CoVantage, LLC

Contents

Acknowledgements	ix
Foreword	xi
JARLATH F. BENSON	
Introduction	1

PART 1
Forming a Group   3

1	Assessment	5
2	Mixed Gender Groups	15
3	The Virtual Group	18
4	Measuring Progress	22
5	Note Keeping	23

PART 2
Therapeutic Co-Working   25

6	Therapeutic Co-Working	27

PART 3
Session Structure   33

7	Session Structure	35

vi Contents

PART 4
Session Themes   41

8 Introductory Session: Confidentiality Contract and Codes of
   Behaviour, Safe Place Visualisation, Art Piece and Discussion   43

9 Self-Soothing   47

10 Boundaries   49

11 Trust and Intimacy   52

12 Self-Assertion / Speaking Your Truth   54

13 The Family of Origin   57

14 Dealing with Tyrants   63

15 Anger / Rage   66

16 Grief and Depression   69

17 Loneliness   72

18 Shame   74

19 Sensuality and Sexuality   78

20 Fear   80

21 Suicidality   83

22 The Myth of Forgiveness   86

23 The Question of Evil   89

24 Brokenness and Healing   92

25 Inner Child Visualisation   94

26 Endings and Beginnings   96

27 Ways Forward   99

28 Closing Session   101

Appendices   103

1 Visualisations and Art Exercises   105

2 Relaxations and Meditations   110

3	Assessment Form	118
4	Referral Form	120
5	Confidentiality Contract	121
6	Invitation Letter	123
7	Information Leaflet	124
8	Eligibility Criteria	127
9	Note-Keeping Template	128
10	Feedback Form	129
	Index	131

Acknowledgements

My primary experience as a group therapist was one in which I was largely along for the ride. I had the great privilege of shadowing my colleague at that time, Mary Rose Kiernan, in working with, assessing, formulating and running a group. Following the departure of this colleague, with the generous support and encouragement of my director of services, Fiona Ward, I was entrusted to grow and develop this method of working independently. I looked to a variety of models on working with trauma and sought to establish a way of working in group that would promote change, growth and a sense of community that was healthy, supportive and educational. I was fortunate to have the peerless guidance of Kay Gilliland, a highly experienced family therapist and senior therapeutic supervisor, whose input and assistance it is impossible to quantify. The resulting model is the fruit of that endeavour which has taken that many years to emerge in a confident form. I have since run this style of group many times within the National Counselling Service and have also run the same model of treatment in private practice. The learning is ongoing and I expect that this will always be the case.

My thanks and appreciation to the many groups I have been privileged to be a member of. My gratitude to the primary group of my family, where more was learned than it would be possible to put into words. My immense appreciation to Akong Rinpoche, Edie Irwin, Dr Brion Sweeney and Stephan Storm for providing the Back to Beginnings and Taming the Tiger group programmes through Tara Rokpa Therapy. This was a formative experience and it has gone on to influence and shape my thinking and approach when working with groups. My thanks to Arwen Dreamwalker for years of guidance and healing groups, her expertise as a Jungian therapist and Medicine Woman is immeasurable and it was an honour to witness such mastery at work. My thanks also to Anja Huikeshoven for the Template Healing groups that I have participated in over the course of many years. My initial scepticism was replaced with a great respect for this way of working in groups and has initiated changes that have been lasting and profound. All of these transformative group experiences have been impactful in ways it would be impossible to take the true measure of. They have all been influential in guiding my path personally and professionally to a great degree.

x Acknowledgements

My thanks to Jarlath Benson, from whom I was fortunate to receive provocative and stimulating group training and input over recent years. My thanks to the colleagues who have co-facilitated groups with me over the past 20 years: Mary Rose Kiernan, Brian Ryle, Laura O Connor, Romy Paust and Patricia Newham. It has been a pleasure to have the support and input of their perspective and enthusiasm for the work.

I have been informed over the years by many people and many influences but none more so than the many clients I have had the honour to work with both in an individual and a group context. Any understanding that I have gained of the dynamics of surviving abuse, and the tremendous courage, ingenuity and resilience that it takes to do so, is principally as result of the bravery of those individuals. Their risk in breaking the secrecy they had been indoctrinated into is both the spirit and the ink of this book. I hope that this book encourages therapists to risk similarly and embrace working in a group context with this rich and resourceful client group.

Thank you most of all to Lilly and Eve, who allowed me to disappear in the evenings to write this book and who are the most treasured group that I am a member of.

Foreword

Jarlath F. Benson

What a daring and incredibly important healing there is in bringing people into a therapeutic workgroup who may have had abusive and traumatic experiences in previous groups or may have intense social problems as a consequence of betrayal that can make group membership terribly difficult or threatening. The nature of trauma and abuse means that the ordinary and human experience of relationship, intimacy and contact is violated and betrayed and the subsequent internal psychological structures which are essential to create a secure sense of self safely attached to others is severely compromised.

How courageous then must the participants and facilitators be to involve themselves in a group modality that by its nature must stir up a whole range of anxieties and interpersonal tensions.

The group is such a very public space with multiple opportunities for blaming and shaming to take place and inevitably this can and will agitate and trigger anxieties and concerns to do with loss of face, criticism, rejection, scapegoating, competition, rivalry, envy and a plethora of social tensions and emotions.

To join to the group and make a commitment to attend and not to flee the potentially threatening relationships, as previously they might have done, activates members' anxieties and sets off their typical devices for avoiding intimacy and sabotaging relationships in order not to be broken and betrayed again.

And yet it is precisely that capacity of the group work modality to heal where previously individual, family and community could not hold and became pernicious that Lorraine McColgan in this text so ably and vividly describes and highlights. It is clear that she believes that many survivors of abuse have been disabled by what she calls a pseudo-familial context and that for this population a therapeutic group can offer a "supportive, clean, honest, boundaried and clear" opportunity to "recast their mental and emotional template".

McColgan offers a practical guide to therapeutic group work for mental health professionals who work with adult survivors of sexual abuse. Her therapeutic group work synthesises a psychoeducational approach with a dynamic process perspective and mindfulness techniques derived from her own Buddhist practice.

She guides the practitioner through the steps required to establish and facilitate a group in this modality and explores the values, rationale and meaning which underpin her work. She addresses the thorny problems of assessment and group composition and considers the possibilities and pitfalls of co-leadership.

McColgan then sets out 21 sessions which from her experience are most suitable to deal with the intra-psychic and inter-personal ruptures, griefs and losses of the traumatised and betrayed. These sessions are thematic but provide ample opportunity for dynamic and extemporaneous interactions and exploration.

These sessions range from participants' experiences of boundaries, to dealing with tyrants, the central experience of shame and disgust and the intimate and ubiquitous issues to do with suicidality. There is help to learn how to self-soothe, transformative possibilities to repair trust and intimacy and deep reflection on the myth of forgiveness and the question of evil.

She creates a consistent and predictable structure to the group life cycle and to each session which builds confidence and allows participants to self-reveal and explore at their own pace. An interesting set of appendices at the end offers practitioners materials in the form of various art exercises and visualisations that can be used and a series of examples of governance forms to contain and hold the group and its work.

I like this work. It is simple but profound. Unpretentious and eminently usable. I would recommend this text for the beginner who could easily benefit from being gently and wisely led through a course of group work by this text and also for more seasoned practitioners for whom the text would provide a very welcome template that can be adjusted to their level and skill.

But above all thank you Lorraine for the insight and daring to utilise the public forum of group work to bring the shamed and betrayed back to social interaction and connection.

May Day 2021

Introduction

This book was written, much as the groups I have conducted over a 20-year period, as a response to the needs of the community of adults who have survived experiences of abuse as children. These abuses include those of a violent, sexual and emotional nature and also the often under reported experiences of neglect. I have conducted these groups both in a public health and private setting. In my private practice I have worked as a solo therapist, while in the public health setting, for the Health Service Executive in the North East of Ireland, I have worked in all of my groups with a variety of co-therapists, all of whom were my valued colleagues within the service. For the purpose of confidentiality, I have drawn all of my examples in the text solely from my private practice and have altered all identifying details.

This book aims to provide a clear and comprehensive original group treatment model for adult survivors of childhood abuse. It guides the practitioner through the steps of establishing and running a group in this modality and explores the underpinning values, rationale and meaning inherent in engaging in this undertaking. It provides all the necessary tools for its execution and it is my hope that this enables the book to be used directly as a manual for clinicians and to allow them to engage in this way of working without delay.

There is a synthesis of an educational and a process model that evolves from the need to be clear about the dynamics of abuse and to also apply that understanding to one's own personal story and to that of others. The hidden nature of abuse is a significant element of its power. Working in a group addresses that very secrecy in an immediate and direct way and in so doing seeks to undo the shame that secrecy holds. It is hoped that the understanding gained from this work will help to establish group work as the optimum matrix for effecting change with this client population and may help to establish group work as best practice within the institutions that provide for their care.

Sources of influence range from Buddhist schools of thought and contemplative philosophies to traditional psychological theory and psychoanalytic tenets of group practice. While strongly guided by psychoanalytic principals that relate to group formation, assessment and dynamic relational issues, a "pure"

DOI: 10.4324/9781003268888-1

psychoanalytic model required additional and necessary educational pieces of work and so an original model emerged to encompass these elements.

At the heart of the work, there is an understanding of the loss of community for many individuals who have experienced abuse and trauma, a lack of being able to speak openly of their experiences and to be heard and accepted. My wish was to provide a healthy, reflective and robust framework in which to authentically address themes which are central to humanity. The experience of abuse and trauma often serves to highlight these themes and to lend urgency to understanding them as a way of reinstating meaning in lives that have had their sense of meaning, justice and truth badly shaken.

Part I

Forming a Group

Chapter 1

Assessment

Choosing the members of a therapeutic group is perhaps the most important and crucial aspect to get right. When a group gels and acts as a supportive and reflective and safely challenging space, there is nothing as effective for the promotion of profound and positive change. If there is a misstep at this point, and an unsuitable person or persons are admitted to the group, you will have considerably reduced the efficacy of the work, if not effectively sabotaged it.

A client population that has survived the experience of trauma and abuse has often done so within a family or pseudo-familial context. The experience of participating in the therapeutic group should in no way echo those early group memberships and rather should be wholly supportive, clean, honest, boundaried and clear. The desire is to create a healthily functioning community where the traumatised client can recast their mental and emotional template of this intimate environment. Assagioli speaks of the group as a place where people can begin to practice "right relations" and to form a clearer understanding of the practice and function of this way of relating (Assagioli, 1983, p.27). As a consequence of this internalised new framework they should be endowed with greater clarity, trust and robustness within their own families and communities. Admitting a member who is unable to adhere to the principles, boundaries and spirit of the group, for reasons of motivation, personal development or location in their personal journey, is at best ill-informed and at worst damaging.

Choosing members who are genuinely eligible and able for this type of work is the first act of respect that you demonstrate to the group. It is the foundation for the trust that you are hoping to provide them the experience of. Survivors of trauma and abuse have a near psychic ability to intuit anything or anyone that is potentially tricky or divisive and it reflects poorly on the therapist if they appear to have "missed it". This is an impossible thing for any group member to speak of or address, as it is damning to both the therapist and the fellow group member and so it cannot be processed safely or at all. As there is little or no therapeutic benefit to working through this issue, the best course is to avoid it.

The appropriate number for a group of this nature is from six to eight people, excluding the therapists. This allows sufficient time for all members to have

DOI: 10.4324/9781003268888-3

space, without the room being so full that it becomes difficult to hide or to find a way in. There is a mirroring of the family system contained within this size of a gathering that is beneficial to the processing of this dynamic as it will play out in the group. Too many participants and things become unwieldy and more difficult to guide whereas too few participants will create a vacuum of personalities and compromise the push and pull of the interaction; as Yalom notes, "A critical mass is required for an aggregation of individuals to become an interacting group" (Yalom, 1970, p.31).

Criteria for Eligibility

Finding group members who are ready and able for this type of process is central to creating a fertile and healing dynamic. It is a strong and potent matrix to place the individual client within and proper care must be taken that there is sufficient ego strength and resilience to manage it. The client is not expected to be without vulnerabilities or to have achieved clarity on all matters; nonetheless, it is important that the client who will participate in the group process has done a number of things prior to being considered for this therapeutic milieu.

Commonality

Yalom establishes group cohesiveness as one of the founding elements in the formation of any group. He illustrates that "Those with a greater sense of solidarity or we-ness value the group more highly and will defend it against internal and external threats; voluntary attendance, participation, mutual help, defence of group standards are all greater" (Yalom, 1970, p.31). The client must fit the criteria of the group. It must be clear from the outset what this group is and who it is for. Safety is in some sense provided by a sense of commonality of experience. This enables members to know that they will not stick out or be on their own, as was their early experience. This is half of the battle already, as the profound isolation felt by many as being the only one to whom bad and unspeakable things were happening has created a sense of difference or otherness that has remained with them throughout their lives. The very act of sitting in a room with people who shared similar experiences resets the clock. It is evident that the other participants seem and are normal and do not in any way stand out or appear to be marked by their lives in any observable way. The "weirdness" is neutralised in a single stroke.

Attendance and Punctuality

It is crucial that any client being considered for group has demonstrated an ability to attend regularly for their appointments and to do so in a punctual manner. This demonstrates a sufficiently good level of time and life management, good

Assessment 7

motivation and importantly respect for the therapist and the therapeutic process. Failure to attend regularly and in a timely manner can be read by the group, correctly or otherwise, as disrespectful and can be disruptive to fostering the needed sense of trust and consistency.

A Significant Piece of One-to-One Work Should Have Been Accomplished

Clients should have engaged, in general, in a medium- to long-term therapeutic process. This will have allowed them to form and experience a therapeutic relationship. It should have fostered a level of trust and the ability to reflect on their personal psychological and emotional processes and on their own role in relationship dynamics. Hopefully, this has led to some changes in personal style or behaviour to a greater or lesser degree and if it has not, the therapist should feel that the client is at the tipping point of change and that the group would be an effective catalyst.

This should involve achieving a relatively honest and truthful look at the family of origin as well as the perpetrator(s) of abuse. This is important as it would be highly provocative to a group who have acknowledged the inappropriateness of abuse to have a member who is highly ambivalent or affectionate in their feelings towards a perpetrator. It recreates echoes of the original denial and ignorance that survivors are often met with. To encounter it again in this environment would be highly charged and carry a number of negative consequences. It can risk alienating the group member who carried the ambivalence and potentially turn them into a target for hatred or negative feelings. It may also be seen to reflect poorly on the therapeutic process that had been engaged in, as the therapist "hadn't made them see" how any loyalty to the abuser is "bad" or "wrong".

Some ambivalence is tolerable, however, as most survivors who experienced their abuse within a family context are likely to have it. Intolerance for any closeness to a perpetrator, especially a family member, denies shades of grey, and often the client who is most obviously ambivalent is a soft target for the shadow of the ambivalence that lies within most survivors if the perpetrator was a member of the family of origin. Provocation is not negative and provides fuel for this very valuable theme to be drawn out. Once there is no significant idealisation of the perpetrator these themes are workable within a group context.

Transference issues should have been experienced and resolved successfully. This is an important piece as many clients of a service working with trauma and abuse will have experience neglect, mistrust and manipulation in their primary relationships. As a result of this, many quite understandably face into other relationships with a foundation of mistrust and suspicion and a personal style of defensiveness that echoes the style that they had to adopt in their early years in order to survive and withstand the blows that came to them. In all therapeutic work of any quality, this style will need to be uncovered, faced and, as a result,

8   Forming a Group

modified. It is best if this has been brought into awareness to some degree prior to group entry as an overly defended style will be antagonistic in the group context and has much potential to block safety and trust.

Motivation and Clarity of Purpose

Clients who are volunteering to take the great risk of revealing themselves and their closely guarded secrets and shame, to what, in the beginning, is a group of strangers, should have some sense of why they are doing it. They will of course have been sold the idea by their therapist but it is important that they have identified some tangible potential benefit for themselves. Most frequently, a reduction in isolation is identifiable as a benefit. Other gains are increased self-esteem, self-assertiveness and increases in clarity and direction. It is not of benefit if a client is participating solely on the direction of the therapist and simply being a good client and doing what is suggested. Some nugget of personal price will be instrumental in making the investment in the process.

Unsuitable Clients

As has already been stated, a rogue participant can cause significant disruption to the forming and successful execution of a therapeutic group. Clients with certain characteristics simply do not suit this process and will not benefit personally from it nor bring benefit to others. As therapists we can often like certain clients or possess an empathy for them and their situations that can make us desirous of their inclusion in a group. At times we can have clients who have not moved on and that we might like to wash our hands of, and referral to a group may seem to be a solution.

Group referral, however, is no place for indulging either preferential treatment or burnout. As Benson states, "If members are to achieve personal goals and help accomplish the group task they require a healthy environment which encourages them to have intimate relationships with each other and fosters independence" (Benson, 1987, p.169). The cost is high for all if an unsuitable candidate enters the group with much of the group's time and resources being hijacked by the individual in question. This leads to resentment on the part of the majority of participants who would like to "get on with it" and, quite correctly, do not wish to spend time fire fighting one group member's negative behaviour and influence. The following list outlines who is unsuitable and why this is the case.

Clients with Active Addiction Issues

Those clients who are actively engaged in issues of addiction, that are obvious to observe and evidently harmful, are not sufficiently stable to engage in group. The use and misuse of any substance to control or modify emotion is indicative of a lack of ability and/or motivation to substantially face or address said emotions.

As this is the very process that underpins the working of therapy, it is crucial that it can be managed by all participants. Groups that work primarily with issues of addiction are far more suitable for this type of client.

I refer principally here to drugs and alcohol and sexual addictions. Other addictions are potentially more workable in the group context. Gambling and eating addictions that are not life or lifestyle threatening may be sufficiently mild that they can be workable and should not be immediate criteria for exclusion. Many clients will engage in self-soothing behaviour that has a negative consequence – indeed, this topic is included in the group work. Very fruitful sessions can emerge from sharing experiences of comfort eating and drinking and self-medication with prescription medicines, and to the extent that shame and secrecy can be lifted in these areas, real transformations can be made. It is common also that alcohol and prescription medication can be used as a self-soothing device by many clients, indeed by many individuals who have no need of therapy, and it is a question of degree and level of impact of this behaviour that determines suitability or otherwise.

Clients with Diagnosis of Borderline, Schizophrenic or Other Personality Disorders

Clients who present within the spectrum of the personality disorders, as outlined by DSM, are not eligible candidates for inclusion on this type of group. This client group typically demonstrates symptomology that speaks of a core instability that is too great to be managed in this model of group therapy. Medication is central to the regulation of the symptoms that present with this population and individual therapeutic intervention is more suitable. Clients who have had a diagnosis of bipolar or manic depression in the past but who have been stable for a consistent time period should be able to engage providing they meet the other outlined criteria. It should be noted, however, that participation could trigger a temporary resurfacing of old symptoms and provision and assistance should be made available for this.

Actively Traumatised Clients

Clients who have undergone a recent trauma or significant loss or who experience vivid flashbacks to the extent that they are immobilising to them may find the group setting too provocative and triggering. It is not advantageous to these clients to have "too much too soon" and the experience of having a flashback that has a physical affect in a group setting may be overwhelming for both that client and the group, not to mention the therapist. All clients should have the ability to a large extent to contain strong emotion (which does not mean not to express it) in a manner that does not cause concern for their physical or mental wellbeing. It is preferable if there has been some (it need not be complete) integration of trauma, as wholly unprocessed trauma in a group context can feel dangerous.

Narcissistic Clients

This may be but is not exclusively characterised as a personality disorder. The narcissistic personality is a disorder in which people have an inflated sense of their own importance, a deep need for admiration and a lack of empathy for others. Beneath this presentation lies a fragile self-esteem that's highly vulnerable and reactive to criticism. Clients who exhibit these traits are most likely poor candidates for therapy as they frequently do not consider themselves to have a problem and instead project any shadow thoughts or feelings outwards. It is very difficult to treat clients with these symptoms individually but their inclusion in a group will only result in sabotage and discord as they are most likely to be hostile to the challenges that will inevitably come to them in this setting.

Perpetrators of Abuse

Clients who actively engage in the perpetrating or perpetuating of any ongoing treatment of abuse should not be included. As stated, clarity on the unacceptability of abuse is a criterion for inclusion and any client who engages in abusive behaviour does not meet the eligibility criteria. There can be subtleties to this however and what is a norm in one family context may be viewed as an abuse in another. Clients may differ over such issues of parenting style as acceptable curfews, diet, verbal reproofs and sibling rivalry. These again can be useful topics to draw out, however abuse in this context refers to the conscious and deliberate knowledge of or participation in what constitutes a clear abuse of a minor.

Clients Who Are Not Punctual or Good Attendees

Clients who have not demonstrated an ability to make a commitment to regular and timely attendance should not be considered suitable. Central to the smooth and effective running of the group is the consistency of all of the members. This consistency at its most basic refers to being regularly present and being on time.

Referral to Group

It is a good idea to have a clear referral form for all therapists who wish to refer in to a group (see Appendix 4). This guides the thinking of the referral agent as it will indicate the areas of work that should have been addressed prior to considering referral. It is helpful also to furnish referral agents with an information leaflet and eligibility criteria to best guide them in choosing appropriate candidates (see Appendix 7).

The Process of Assessment

Introducing the idea of participation in a therapeutic group is a matter of timing. There is a point where a significant chunk of work has been accomplished and tangible gains have been made, however the client may still lack friendships or a social network of any substance or feel that while they have been seen and understood in the therapeutic relationship, this remains a rarefied experience. It is useful at this stage to begin to explore the widening of this experience into a community setting. This has the advantage of dissolving any myths that it is only possible to be "met" by a mental health professional, due to the indigestible nature of one's story.

Many clients feel that they are hiding large aspects of themselves and their histories to those close to them and as a consequence, intimacy has been compromised in their lives. The one-to-one therapy should shift this dynamic and shrink the tyranny of shame and secrecy to a good degree. Once this coup has been accomplished it makes sense to capitalise on it. If the therapeutic relationship has been a positive one it is a strong platform for recommending the continuation of the clients' transformative process in a group setting.

The therapist is a trusted figure who would not make any suggestion that is not in the client's interest. The process of referral is more straightforward if the same therapist is also going to be the group therapist. This allows for a continuation and further development of the original working alliance and the therapist can function as an anchor or "safety person" enabling the transition to be less anxiety provoking. If the movement is to a different therapist, it will be necessary to do a piece of bridging work with the new therapist prior to the commencement of the group. It is an intimidating thing to walk into a room full of strangers for the most neutral of topics or agendas, but for a group working with issues of abuse, it is too frightening and provocative to do without a link person.

Preparation for the group is an important process and one worth doing well. If this piece is successfully bridged, in my experience, the group can hit the ground running, and gain the optimum benefit from their time.

Referring One's Own Client to One's Own Group

Referring a client whom you have worked with over a period of time to a group that you are facilitating should be an organic movement. You know the client meets the eligibility criteria and is an appropriate candidate. The client is well known to you, as are you to them, and the transition contains a measure of familiarity as well as one of onward development. The established relationship and structure of therapy provides the ideal milieu for the therapist to explain and explore the potential benefits of participation in the group and for the client to address any concerns or anxieties. It is straightforward to illustrate the format and purpose of the group and so the preparation work should occur seamlessly.

It can still feel a little jarring or alarming for the client to have this movement proposed. As this proposition only comes at a time when the client is easing out of one-to-one therapy, it should not be experienced too much as a rejection, particularly as the therapist themselves will be remaining in situ. It is however, a sharing of a special relationship with others and an acknowledgement that the therapist

12 Forming a Group

has special relationships with others besides the client. This has the potential to illicit old feelings of sibling rivalry, however this should be containable due to the substance of the one-to-one work, and the more gross neurotic aspects should not be at such a level as to poison the waters of the group endeavour.

Preparation here involves describing the function and purpose of the group, outlining its structure and the benefits as you perceive them. There is a degree of "selling" the group, although in my experience this usually pertains to anxieties about speaking in front of a crowd and possibly knowing another group member. It should not be necessary to have to do a hard sell to existing clients, as they should have a personal readiness for this style of engagement and to some extent be able to discern the benefits for themselves.

Assessing a Client from a Colleague

The process of assessment and preparation with a client who has been referred by a colleague involves more groundwork. In the previous case the assessment for eligibility had been an ongoing process that occurred over the duration of the individual work whereas this is not the case with an external referral. While colleagues should have been furnished with the eligibility criteria and have a good understanding of what constitutes an appropriate referral, this may not always be the case and cannot be assumed to be so.

Any colleague wishing to refer should be given the full details and information on the type and nature of group that you are running and be supplied with a referral form. The form itself should help guide thinking in relation to the appropriateness of the recommendation (see Appendix 4). The referring therapist should be clear with the client they are referring that the referral is for assessment only and that while they think it might be of benefit to them, it is the group therapist who will make the determination. The therapist should explain to the client that this may be for a number of reasons including available spaces, suitability and other practicalities. It is important that the client who may, in the end, be deemed not suitable have no flavour of having been rejected or perceived as "not good enough" to make it into the group, and it is necessary for the referral agent to be very clear on this point with their client. It is always useful to speak with the referring agent about the client as they will be able to identify the particular qualities of that client that the client might themselves not volunteer. They should also be able to highlight areas of tension or family dynamics that might be informative.

Conducting the Assessment

Once the client has been proposed and appears at an initial stage to be a suitable candidate, the therapist or co-therapists should arrange a meeting with them for an assessment. The assessment form should be completed at this meeting (see Appendix 3), and if the client is appropriate for group, this meeting should serve as an introduction to the therapists who will be running the group and provide a good general sense of the style, purpose and ethos of the group. It is best if the client meets with both therapists if it is a group run by two therapists. The principal therapist should perform the assessment with the co-therapist shadowing and contributing where the client has questions or concerns.

The assessment form should explore the issues that relate to the eligibility criteria as well as examining the client's experience of groups and group dynamics. Such issues as how they tend to position themselves in group setting (are they the shy one, the gregarious one, the facilitator etc.) and where they might like this to be different in the future. It is helpful to explore school and community groupings as well as that of the primary group, the family. It is useful to try to elicit what their communication style is and if they have an awareness of this. It is most useful to identify any negative group experiences at this stage and to allow the client to voice their fears of their re-occurrence as the airing of these themes is a significant relief for the client and the best method of preventing an unconscious acting out of an old and unhelpful scenario.

This meeting serves also as a meeting and bridging point for the client with the new therapists and should be informative and reassuring for them. In short, this meeting should further encourage the client and add an increased sense of clarity and purpose about their upcoming involvement with the group process. The client should be furnished with the group information leaflet at the close of this session, so as to have something tangible to take away with them and which reinforces the information that they have just received. They should be invited to contact the therapists if they should have any further questions or concerns prior to the commencement of group therapy. They should at that point be given the start date of the group and the time and location details. If these have not been established, it will be necessary to write to them with those details relatively quickly following this meeting. This helps to make the upcoming venture a reality and to bed it down more deeply into consciousness. Where possible, it is best to have this meeting in the venue where the group will be taking place, as it establishes familiarity and removes mystery and fear. It also helps to visualise the location in the imagining of the process and helps establish the link and begin the process before it starts proper.

If the client is not deemed suitable at the time of assessment, it is best to let them know that is your assessment and why. This should be framed in such a way that affirms the client in who and how they are and carries no shadow of judgement or sense of falling short. Common reasons for unsuitability are to do with timing issues and ability to commit on a consistent basis. Life events can overtake any client's plans and rather than trying to make something work when it will be difficult and possible stressful, it might be best to wait for a more beneficial time in the client's life to engage in such fruitful work so as to gain the full benefit.

The assessing therapist may ascertain, despite the client having engaged in long-term work and seeming on paper to fit the eligibility criteria, that there are

14 Forming a Group

still significant personal and developmental issues that would render the client unsuitable for group. In these instances, it is useful to gently map out the reasons why the group may be overwhelming or potentially destabilising for that individual. A lack of inclusion in those cases is then possible to be framed as an act of care or kindness to the client as a result of thoroughly considering their circumstances. It is necessary to bridge this back to the referring agent and outline the reasons for the decision. The referral agent may need to alter their treatment plan for that client and will need to be informed without delay. The conversation of why the client was unsuitable is also a useful part of the process of ongoing clarification and peer education about the function and purpose of group therapy, and it is important to take the time to do these pieces of work thoroughly and with care.

References

Assagioli, R. (1983) *Psychosynthesis Typology: Psychosynthesis Monograph*. London: Institute of Psychosynthesis.

Benson, J.F. (1987) *Working More Creatively With Groups*. London: Routledge.

Yalom, I.D. (1970) *The Theory and Practice of Group Psychotherapy*. New York: Basic Books.

Chapter 2

Mixed Gender Groups

I recall setting out on my first mission as a fledgling group therapist. My fear levels were high and were matched only by a desire to get this right and above all, to harm no one in the process. This, well intended but perhaps hyper, vigilance had made me feel that it would not be tolerable for the group to have members of the opposite sex. In the case of most therapeutic services, which are predominantly female in constitution, this meant no men. My first groups were single sex as a result of my own fears that I may re-traumatise the women of the group as most of their perpetrators had been male. This was a well-meaning decision and had its origin in the attempt to vouchsafe the least provocative environment for healing to occur and to provide an optimum sense of safety.

As time passed and my own confidence as a group therapist grew I relaxed this position considerably, prompted by the clients' levels of growth, engagement and ability for the process. Male clients who were eminently suited began to present themselves both privately and within the health service, so that it began to seem discriminating to continue to omit them. There was also an opportunity to show women that men also suffered abuse, sometimes at the hands of women and mothers, and to remove any assumption that perpetrators or survivors typically fall into one gender or the other. The fact that there were insufficient men to constitute a group of their own necessitated a definite move away from a single sex model.

As Mike Lew says in his work *Victims No Longer*, "the effects of abuse are equally profound whether one is male or female", and he notes "they are also generally similar". Lew (1993, p.38). Lew writes that the expectations placed on the genders may well be different, however, and explores the differences of the impact of being a "victim" on the two sexes (Lew, 1993). Rich understanding and meaningful exchanges can occur in teasing out these differences and group members can see more deeply how these roles have played into their own reactions and responses. Men typically note that it is not acceptable to have been victimised and reflect that it was their belief that "a real man is expected to protect himself in any situation. He is supposed to solve any problem and recover from any setback" (Lew, 1993, p.41). It is helpful to look at the impossibility of this position in the

DOI: 10.4324/9781003268888-4

16 Forming a Group

group and for some of the myths that artificially divide the sexes to be debunked. It is often useful for men to see that many of the women had received the exact same message in handling their own experiences of abuse and for all to acknowledge the damage of having been emotionally silenced and to navigate a pathway out of it.

Preparation that is done prior to joining the group should identify if potential members feel that they would have difficulty or be triggered in any way by the presence of the opposite gender. This may be workable in the individual therapy sessions and can be reframed as an opportunity to make an alternative experience in a context of safety that it may be hard to equal outside of a therapeutic environment. If this feeling of risk is possible to challenge it is a unique chance to tackle and transform perceptions that have become stuck. Some clients may feel that this is too charged for them and that it would simply not be possible to overcome their anxiety and heightened sense of vulnerability. This is important to hear and respect. There are many ways of working in a group and the same sex matrices may feel like the only sufficiently comfortable way of working for some.

For some of the women of the group, it can be surprising that boys are victims of abuse. I have heard more than once in group settings from women who expressed gratitude that their children had been male as they felt this conferred a greater degree of safety to them. As this notion dissolves members can come to see how male family members, whom they would have thought to be immune, may also have been targets of abuse. This can have the effect of promoting conversations and insight outside of the room and in some cases has altered and healed sibling relationships.

Some of the male members who suffered at the hands of their mothers are moved by the positive mothering that they hear from the women in the group. The same is true in relation to fathering. This disproves an often-tacit belief in some central "badness" or untrustworthiness in the opposite sex and opens the ground to a meaningful dialogue between the two perspectives. Members realise, more often than not, how little essential difference there really is. Humanity, understanding, compassion and insight are transformative wherever we encounter them.

Perpetrators, as well as survivors, can be of either gender. The primary narrative of sexual abuse refers to the abuse of girls or boys by adult or near adult men. Less often is sexual abuse by women discussed or even mentioned. This might be the ultimate taboo; however, it may well be more frequent than is imagined. If a society lacks a language for, or a belief in, the female perpetrator of sexual abuse, then it will be very hard to discuss.

Group members will occupy many roles, their gender being just one. Clients will be mothers, fathers, bosses, coaches, teachers and siblings, any of which may have been the perpetrator for any of the other group members. It is reductive to say that any of these issues would be less provocative than gender. Men are abused by women who are mothers, sisters, relatives or trusted adults, as girls can be by fathers, brothers, relatives or trusted men. Culpability is not embedded within any particular gender or sexual identity but in the wilful and knowing transgression of a child's person. The opportunity to establish new pathways and understandings with the opposite or same sex is a valuable outcome of bringing men and women together in undertaking this work.

Reference

Lew, M. (1993) *Victims No Longer: A Guide for Men Recovering from Child Sexual Abuse.* London: Cedar.

Chapter 3

The Virtual Group

To say that my original position on conducting a group in a virtual format was contrary would be a significant understatement. As a therapeutic milieu, the group signifies a place for new relationships, communication styles, interpersonal growth and intimacy that seemed to very clearly require a physical environment. I had always carried the assumption that, without this physicality, the work simply could not be done. I would not have designed or commenced a virtual group and indeed I had met, as had many of my colleagues, suggestions of virtual working with some judgement and even derision. This was the case in a time when one had the luxury of choice and during the writing of this book, that luxury was withdrawn.

All of humanity has been required to come together as a group in order to vouchsafe our physical survival and our experience of contact and physicality has been revolutionised to a previously unimaginable degree. Virtual contact has quickly become the primary form of meeting in every aspect of work, social and leisure activity. Web-based meeting platforms, whilst not new to many in a work setting, became mandatory for all and quickly established themselves as the primary place of socialisation. This was a steep learning curve for many and placed a standard of technological competence and fluency front and centre in the life of most individuals. It allowed the possibility to meet en masse where this would not have otherwise been possible and facilitated groups of all types to meet and communicate as they would have prior to having to negotiate a global pandemic.

Web-based formats are in wide supply and once you have satisfied yourself and your organisation as to the security of the platform, set up and invitation to the meeting is relatively straightforward. If the therapists have any resistance to technology, now is the time to challenge this, as this way of working is now a necessity and not an option. Teleconference modalities can also be effective and indeed can have a clearer sound at times, however having sound and picture is far preferable in reducing the sense of distance and difference.

The therapeutic group is no exception to these changes and developments and it was to my great surprise that I experienced this work running successfully and

DOI: 10.4324/9781003268888-5

beneficially through web-based working. For those groups that were already in existence and had to move to a virtual arena, the shift was helped by the substance of the relationships and communications already lived in the room. This substance was more easily transportable despite some initial resistance and comparison to better days. Acknowledging the loss of what was and allowing space for feelings of disgruntlement and grief is important and necessary. This acknowledgement relates to both the therapeutic group specifically but also to the same loss that is being experienced in all relationships and groups and as such is material to be richly mined and examined in the work of the group.

For groups that are being established virtually from the beginning there is a different challenge to work with as there is no previous pot to draw from and the screen is the only place where the group experience will occur. The group, however, should proceed in exactly the same manner as though it was happening in the room. The model of group work does not require any fundamental reinvention, but rather benefits from attention to certain areas in advance. Additional preparation must be done regarding technological issues and in order to ensure that all participants have secured a safe and private space that will remain secure for the duration of the session. Additional conversations will be needed with participants individually to address this style of working and to answer any concerns that this raises.

There is a measure of nurture that the therapists would have provided that participants will now have to source for themselves. Participants will need to access their own pillows and blankets for the relaxations and meditations, ensure their own comfort and secure the boundaries of their own session. For those who have had this modelled in the physical group, it is quite straightforward to continue individually what has been experienced collectively, although there will still need to be some effort made, but for those to whom it is new, these matters will need to be made explicit. To this end, additional contracting is needed that specifically addresses the matters of concern when working virtually.

The contract provides an additional psychological skin around the group (Benson, 2019) and echoes the shape of the boundaries and codes of conduct established in the original contract whilst making more specific certain aspects of good manners that participants will have to bear in mind when operating from their own homes. Members are asked to attend to the privacy of other members, who will be appearing on the screen in locations beyond their control. It is important that everyone understands that they are now being trusted with the privacy of others in a concrete way and that ensuring and protecting this privacy is fundamental. If members have others appearing in the background or entering the room, this is a breach of confidentiality and appropriate steps need to be taken to ensure that this does not occur. If any member requires help from a friend or family member to set up initially, they must arrange this ahead of time or discuss this with the therapist who can assist them with any concerns.

20 Forming a Group

Members are also encouraged to dress and present themselves as though they were attending in person. The tendency for people to become more casual than they would customarily be as a result of not leaving the house can have the feel of a lack of effort or a subtle disrespect and it is relevant to make this overt and to set an atmospheric tone as well as a practical one.

It is not always possible to legislate for every eventuality when the group is off site in this way and it will be likely that door bells will ring and physical intrusions that could not have been predicted will occur. This, as they say, is life, and as long as every effort has been made and every participant has sought in earnest to seal their perimeter, there will be a need to roll with the punches at times. Technological glitches can create the same feeling of disruption and frustration and it is again likely that pictures and sound will come and go intermittently on occasion. This is certainly difficult for participants and therapists alike and can have the effect of silencing and sabotaging members. It is important to name these frustrations and effects so that they are neutralised as effectively as possible and don't linger as unmentioned obstacles.

It is important to address the lack of physicality and the experience of this. This is a shared experience and participants may note that it is not possible to make eye contact, read body language or "get a sense" of people in the same way. While members may not want to touch one another, they cannot offer a tissue to someone who is upset or put a comforting hand on them. There is also, at the current time, the wider context of all physical contact having been reduced due to its risk of spreading contagion. What is felt in the group is being felt more generally and the discussion of how it is experienced in the group has wider references which it can be fruitful to explore. For many who are living and feeling this adjustment and isolation in real time, there is the opportunity to speak about that and to locate the particular dilemmas and discomforts that accompany this. The group might look at how they can touch one another with words and examine how intimacy can still develop through the attention and support we can lend to one another.

There can be an inadvertent mirroring of the experience of having had to live with abuse in the glitches and disruptions to communication. The sense of trying to speak and being cut off or not understood on crucial communication and sharing can be re-enacted if the sound or picture goes at the wrong time. It is important to name this and attend to it within the group framework so that this sense does not intrude detrimentally on the work of the group.

There are two questions at the heart of conducting a group remotely. The first is practical and addresses the technological requirements necessary to facilitate the meeting. There will undoubtedly be niggles and obstacles with this and even when the platform is well established, the boundary can be compromised by failures of reception and uncontrollable factors impinging on the flow of expression and communication. This will come and go and can be acknowledged and accommodated if everyone keeps their cool and accepts that the platform is occasionally imperfect. The second and more far-reaching concern is whether the platform can hold emotional space for strong and difficult feelings to be expressed and shared. It is one thing to risk visible upset and distress when in a room where others may reach out physically (although they typically do not in any demonstrative way) and to do so where no one can. The feeling of risk can be great, as the remoteness can be even more deeply felt in the silence that occurs at a distance. There can be a sense of keeping things safe enough for the format and it will be important to challenge this and for members to risk messy expression and emotion and see and feel that it can be held through the screen. I have found that it can indeed be immaculately held and that a realness of intimacy and connection can be fostered and built upon despite the physical distance. I have witnessed this to be profoundly healing and supportive to those in isolated circumstances and in a world where this is precisely the type of experience that is being eroded and compromised.

I have been encouraged well beyond what I would have envisioned possible by my own experiences in working virtually. I have seen groups form, gel, develop, process and meet tasks and challenges in the same way that I have seen them do when together in the room. I have felt the effect of meditation to calm and focus through the screen. I have been moved by the degree to which trust and intimacy have been established and developed in this format and have witnessed the same significant second order change occur for members in their positions, choices and behaviours outside of the group. This way of working offers innovations not previously considered and allows for the inclusion of participants who have physical obstacles in attending or live in remote settings or who are geographically far apart to come together and do the work. In a time where there is an ongoing erosion of the possibility of meeting in groups and a price being paid by the ensuing isolation this creates, it is a privilege to be able to provide this option and to be able to continue to engage in such creative work.

Reference

Benson, J.F. (2019) From training "On working with groups". Drogheda, Ireland, March.

Chapter 4

Measuring Progress

Many agencies require some measurement of the success and efficacy of the helping professions and of the methods engaged with in doing this work. There are a plethora of measurement tools, some of which are free to the public and others which have requirements and need authorisation for their use. Depending on the demands of the service, the clinician can review and decide amongst these options.

The National Counselling Service routinely uses the CORE measure to initially identify issues of risk and to ascertain the progress made in relation to such items as loneliness, relationships, personal efficacy and personal improvement and contentment over the therapeutic time period. This measure is very helpful in noting change and progress and is simple for clients to use and quick to administer.

All measures that calculate statistically can quickly and easily provide a snapshot of the benefits gained and the progress made. This often serves to satisfy organisational requirements in regard to proof of change and measurable improvement and can be most helpful for clients to note their own progress in this easily understood manner.

Qualitative measures glean more detailed information and can capture less tangible elements than may be measured in quantitative tools. I have included a qualitative questionnaire in Appendix 10 which was developed with a view to drawing out participants' sense of what worked for them and why, as well as discovering what they found unhelpful. This feedback can help to inform the development of future group function and polish and refine the basic model as well as facilitating clients to reflect actively on their own journey and process.

DOI: 10.4324/9781003268888-6

Chapter 5

Note Keeping

Different services may have different requirements in relation to note keeping. Group recording presents challenges in capturing both an individual's progress and the movement and themes of the group at large. State organisations may have concerns regarding confidentiality that prevent the recording of clients' details overlapping and being jointly registered on any individual client's notes. This may require that both individual and group records are kept.

Regarding individual notes, one can track the contributions of said client and note any particulars that relate to their own challenges and development. This does not require explicit or identifying information on any other participant and is relatively straightforward. The difficulty with it is that it fails to capture the dynamic process at play and provides little room to refer to the cross play between certain members. This interactive element of the work has a music of its own and often comprises the essence of what is occurring and promoting growth and change.

It is more helpful to use the note-keeping time to reflect with the co-therapist on the themes that emerged, the interacting dyads or triads, any sub-group formations, and commonalities and differences between members in relation to the theme (see Appendix 9). This can be captured in writing or diagrammatically, where there is greater freedom to represent visually the connective arcs between clients on the various aspects. Therapists should also consider how these emerging aspects of dynamic and relationship style may allude to the family of origin, so as to draw this out in the group.

Therapists may consider separately any themes that emerged for them in respect of difficulty or struggle in tracking or understanding the factors at play. They may note any strong reactions they themselves had to any individual or any aspect of the material and register this for useful discussion in their supervision work. It is useful for therapists to see where they had different interpretations of the work and different responses and interventions, as this likely reflects the struggles at play in the room. Differing responses often indicate the therapists being cast in differing roles by group members and this transference and counter transference is rich with meaning and information if the therapists can understand it as such.

DOI: 10.4324/9781003268888-7

Part 2

Therapeutic Co-Working

Chapter 6

Therapeutic Co-Working

It is possible to run this type of group with either one or two therapists. The advantage of running it as an individual therapist is that this avoids potential conflict or ideological clashes with a colleague. It allows the senior practitioner to hold the space comfortably and to focus solely on the dynamics of the group without having to manage the dynamics of the "mini group" of the therapists. This can provide a freedom of practice and expression to the therapist who has had experience in this modality of working and allow them to proceed without having to manage the anxieties and steeper learning curve of the less experienced co-therapist or the differences in approach and interpretation of a peer.

While this may be a seductive reason to proceed alone, there are also disadvantages and missed opportunities in conducting the group as a solo agent. Therapeutic work is largely characterised by privacy and confidentiality. This is a necessary matrix for change to occur within and yet, outside of the supervision process, there is no observation of the therapist's practice. Only in training is the therapist observed and evaluated directly. Once qualified, this ceases to occur. Supervision is an indirect method for maintaining the checks and balances of the therapist's practice and is an effective one, with a good supervisor, for drawing out any blocks, reactivity or obstacles of style that the therapist may be blind to. However, as this method relies solely on the narrative and interpretation of the therapist, it is another experience altogether to have one's practice and interventions seen, in the room, by a colleague. This is the very exposure we are asking the group participants to open themselves up to, so it might be important that we ask the same of ourselves.

Choosing a colleague to co-work with is an interesting process in itself. Often, as groups are established in the framework of a service with a body of staff in the employment of that service, it is from this selection of colleagues that a co-worker must be identified. The first issue you may encounter is that many colleagues may not have a desire to engage in group work. This may be due to a fear of being inexperienced, concerns about holding the therapeutic space for a large number of clients and being overwhelmed, or fears around being seen as a therapist by a colleague. These fears can be allayed by the lead therapist taking the pressure off a

DOI: 10.4324/9781003268888-9

new and less experienced colleague and allowing them to be essentially in the role of a trainee. In this role they can largely observe the lead therapist and make interventions when and if they see fit, with no requirement that they are to guide or master the work. It is then an opportunity for further learning and no expertise is required. At other times, two equally experienced therapists who have not run groups before may confidently enough join forces and run the programme with the support and supervision of an experienced group therapist. It is essential, no matter how experienced the therapists, that group work be supported and guided by an experienced group therapist and supervisor.

The Lead Therapist

The lead therapist occupies a more visible and prominent position at the start of the group, typically (although not always) being the therapist with greater experience and familiarity with the process of working within group settings. This makes it an obvious choice for this therapist to speak more, to introduce the tone and topics of the group and to intervene and guide more directly and overtly than the co-therapist at the start. As noted by Benson, "What distinguishes the leader is the authority given or ascribed to him to influence the group in certain ways, to achieve agreed goals" (Benson, 1987, p.38). He further notes that this authority is required for the task whether the leader likes it or not and that this should not be fudged or denied as a consequence of a lack of personal clarity regarding issues of power and leadership.

It is useful for the group participants to experience some predictability as to who does what in the group space and it allows for the reimagining of the parental dyad in what should be a healthy and functioning model. What is crucial here is that both roles are held by both therapists respectfully and while there may be a difference in position or experience that this is no ground for divisiveness or issues of power to manifest. It is important for both therapists to respect and value one another in their respective roles, which should lend itself to greater flexibility and crossover as time passes in any event. Initially, it is helpful if the lead therapist introduces the themes and speaks to them in a general fashion, so as to direct the group's focus and considerations. They can probe and prompt both individual responses and the group dynamic as they seek to guide reflection, risk taking, identification, separateness and growth. They can help individual members address one another, rather than habitually addressing the therapists, and encourage conversation, challenge and mutuality. The skill required here is in knowing what the group is ready for and when. This is a function of experience and comfort in taking risks where sufficient safety exists for this risk to likely result in growth. Less experienced therapists may feel nervous to risk challenge or to probe too deeply for fear of being intrusive or exposing, and it will feel safer to first gain experience by watching this process and gaining a feel for this more complex manoeuvring.

The Co-Therapist

The role of the co-therapist is to act as ballast and support to the lead therapist and the group. They typically act as a "sweep" and say less up front whilst having a keen eye to the proceedings. They are particularly watchful for anything of note that the lead therapist has perhaps missed or failed to bring in that could usefully be mentioned. The group is such a multi-layered and active space that two therapists are essential in order to catch everything that is unfolding and helpfully work with and contain it. While the lead therapist occupies a more public place and must lead, especially in the beginning stages of the group, the co-therapist is invaluable in monitoring the subtleties that it would be difficult to observe when speaking and directing certain pieces. It is preferable that the co-therapist sits back a little more than the lead in order to observe closely and it is important to balance this with still having a presence in the group. Co-therapists can lead the mediations and visualisations and in so doing have a clear space for their voice and presence. As time goes by and the co-therapists become more confident in the space and in working within a group setting, there can be a more even distribution of tasks and interventions. This should be gradual and smooth and create no sense of territoriality. There is no greater or lesser role, only evolving experience and collaboration.

Supervision

It is essential that all therapists who conduct a group therapeutic process do so under the guidance of a qualified group therapist/supervisor. It is crucial to work in supervision with someone who has a clear knowledge and experience of group dynamics and is aware of the potential pitfalls of communication and the parallel process that is inevitably enacted in this matrix. It has always been true that the efficacy of the therapist correlates strongly with the depth and range of personal work that they have engaged in. This is very clearly so when working therapeutically in groups. The re-enactment of various family dysfunctions, alliances and secrets is often necessary in order for these very dynamics to be clearly seen and worked through.

In the appearance of these matters in the framework of the group the therapists must be very clear in their understanding of their own family situations and be vigilant regarding their own hidden biases and family positions. Patrick Casement helpfully illuminates the role of the *internal supervisor* and highlights the importance of maintaining a high degree of self-awareness throughout. This must exist in addition to formal supervision as there will always be the need to address "the immediacy of the therapeutic present" with the need for the therapist to "remain well disposed towards a patient even when they are being treated as someone with attitudes that may be quite alien" (Casement, 1985, p.29).

It is of the utmost importance for the therapists to communicate openly and honestly regarding their perceptions and how they both feel that thorny issues

30 Therapeutic Co-Working

should be negotiated. Engaging in this work will make it likely that therapists also share their own experiences in their planning and debriefing sessions, as this is what is active in informing how these issues are approached and understood. This has the unique feature of being both personal and professional and has embedded within it the same risk that we ask of our clients.

This parallel process is a feature of therapeutic work and ideally facilitates the therapist's understanding of what this is likely to bring up for members, as they are feeling it to some degree themselves. It is not uncommon for this process to unmask issues that the therapist may not have awareness of and which will therefore feel risky, perhaps to an uncomfortable degree. To this end supervision allows for a safe and professional holding of that and allows the therapist's awareness to unfold and for this to be experienced as a moment of learning and not of judgement, which is exactly what we desire for our clients.

There are many models of supervision, which it would take a separate book to fully explore. I would direct the reader to Page and Wosket's (2001) cyclical model as well as Hawkins and Shohet's (2000) seven eyed model of supervision as instructive, containing and potentially valuable ways of working. I have personally preferred a more conversational and collaborative tone and emphasis in my own supervisory process as this lends itself to greater likelihood of group connectivity, healthy and robust communication and evolving trust and intimacy. I have found more prescriptive models that hold to a tight framework to be at odds with the unfolding of the group experience as they run the risk of fixing and maintaining the position of the power and expertise of the therapist. It is more helpful if this is something that can be challenged and negotiated, both for the group clients with the group therapist and the group therapist with the supervisor.

It is beneficial for supervision on group working to also occur within the context of a group, whether this comprises the lead and co-therapist and supervisor, or open to other colleagues who also run groups. Learning is rich when the context for discussing relational issues is a mirrored environment, and this can foster a greater appreciation of the experience of clients. The unfolding parallel processing requires that a central philosophy of personal risk, respectful communication and honesty must underpin all aspects of the process, as what plays out in the group will very likely play out in the context of the supervision. Jarlath Benson encourages therapists to be willing to fully discuss conflicts and tensions and to be willing to permit and invite differences in style, perception and approach once there is agreement about purpose (Benson, 1987). It is often in the very stuck and blind places, both for therapists and clients, that the alchemical process of the *nigreda* is achieved and potentially resolved, Jung (1959). It is in the successful execution of this transition that *Second Order Change*, as espoused by Watzlavik, Weakland and Fisch in their seminal work *Change: Principles of Problem Formation and Problem Resolution*, is achieved (Watzlavik, Weakland and Fisch, 1974). It is this lasting and meaningful difference and improvement in understanding, behaving and relating that is the goal of this work.

What we learn and, more importantly, how we learn in supervision can feed directly into the therapeutic group, and any gaps or obstacles to health in one part of the system can easily have a domino effect on the other. The skilled therapist and supervisor will have an eye to this and a desire to unmask any sense of blocks or failings, however uncomfortable this may be. It is true that where there is discomfort there is usually growth if this can be tolerated and risked in a respectful climate. I would recommend that both therapists research their supervisor well and both feel happy to engage with them. Supervision is also a process which occurs over time and in which trust builds. There are many groups involved in the running of the therapeutic group and each of these sub-groups mirrors aspects that appear in the primary group, which mirror aspects of the family, which is the primary group for all. A supervisor must have a keen awareness of group dynamics and understand the pathway through difficulties to resolution through effective and responsible communication. It is best if their expertise is based on both a solid and broad ranging theoretical foundation and a strong commitment to their own continuing personal and professional development.

References

Benson, J.F. (1987) *Working More Creatively with Groups*. London: Routledge.

Casement, P. (1985) *On Learning from the Patient*. London: Routledge.

Hawkins, P. and Shohet, R. (2000) *Supervision in the Helping Professions*. Milton Keynes: Open University Press.

Jung, C.J. (1959) *Psychology and Alchemy*. London: Routledge.

Page, S. and Wosket, V. (2001) *Supervising the Counsellor: A Cyclical Model*. London and New York: Routledge.

Watzlavik, P., Weakland, J.H. and Fisch, R. (1974) *Change: Principles of Problem Formation and Problem Resolution*. New York and London: Norton.

Part 3

Session Structure

Chapter 7

Session Structure

Time Frame

This group will occur over the length of 30 sessions, with each session being 90 minutes in duration. It is important that all participants arrive on time so as to make best use of this relatively short window in which to do the work. It is helpful if natural breaks and gaps that will occur can be identified up front and worked into the session as this provides clarity and containment. It is not always possible to have all eventualities covered but the more this is built in to the understanding of the life of the group, the better. It is best if members can identify times they might miss in the future due to pre-arranged appointments and to let the other members know of this. Allowing for these breaks, the length of the group often runs to around nine months, which is interesting in itself. Acknowledging this meaningful span of time allows members to engage consciously from the start in the process of whatever it is they wish to birth for themselves.

Meditation/Visualisation

With the exception of the first session, all sessions should begin with a meditation or visualisation. This should be 20 to 30 minutes in length and mark the opening of each session. Apart from the casual conversation that occurs as members enter and settle into the room, the therapists should, in general, launch the meditation without much or any preamble. The characteristic nervousness and the conversational joviality that often accompanies the beginning of the meetings can seduce the therapist into more talking than is useful at the outset. It is preferable to let members know that all questions and remarks can hold until post meditation as this will result in a more grounded and focused entrance into the work of the session.

Meditation is crucial in both the short and the long term. The immediate effect is to create calm and quiet and to draw members' awareness into the room and into themselves and one another. Background concerns and future plans are disengaged from in a conscious manner so that all can be fully present.

DOI: 10.4324/9781003268888-11

This sets a distinct tone and delineates the space from standard engagements and the rules and habits that accompany them, in an easy and effortless way. Members are noticeably more attuned and available for deeper more considered reflection and responses and the unfolding session is always the richer for it; "when you act out of present moment awareness, whatever you do becomes imbued with a sense of quality, care and love – even the most simple actions" (Tolle, 2005, p.45).

For most participants this is a welcome start, and the benefit is felt quickly. Any anxiety experienced in first engaging in this act of being still and quiet with a room full of relative strangers soon dissipates and members report looking forward to this piece of the work. There may be some members who find the meditations discomforting, or so they believe. In fact, it is not possible for meditation to arouse anxiety or discomfort; rather, it can expose those qualities if they are already present. For some, an underlying state of anxiety is almost a constant feature of their internal landscape and something from which they habitually distract themselves. Engaging in meditation prevents this distraction so that what is present is felt and experienced. It is no wonder that this can then feel discomforting.

It is the job of the therapist to point out this distinction and encourage the client to stretch their tolerance of sitting with this discomfort with a feeling of curiosity. They do not need to seek resolution from the feelings but to learn to relate to them, and to themselves, with less judgement and intolerance. I recall an instance of having to do this myself when studying with Akong Rinpoche, a Buddhist lama and highly regarded meditation teacher. I had been diligently meditating and found that I was encountering high levels of fear. I was sufficiently displeased by this that I took a plane to London, where he was speaking at a public event, to get advice on how best to manage and understand my experience. Having told him of my struggles and experience of fear, he simply said "Good. Just look at it". I was not impressed at the time and lamented having made such a long journey for such little relief. It was only many years later when I realised the wisdom of his instruction. There is no escape from our own minds and whatever they throw up is a direct signpost to wherever it is we are. Our thoughts and emotions drive us relentlessly and can offer little space to acknowledge what is truly before us. As Pema Chodron states in *Start Where You Are*:

> when you feel craving, you could be sitting on the edge of the Grand Canyon, but all you see is this piece of chocolate cake that you are craving. With aversion, you're sitting on the edge of the Grand Canyon, and all you can hear is the angry words you said ten years ago. With ignorance, you are sitting on the edge of the Grand Canyon with a paper bag over your head. Each of these has the power to capture you so completely that you don't even perceive what's in front of you.
>
> (Chodron, 2005, pp.39–40)

Session Structure   37

Typically we look for comfort and good feeling and avoid anything that is unpleasant. What Akong Rinpoche was saying was more profound than I could digest at the time though it was completely correct. If we can make friends with our discomfort and not move off the spot every time we are provoked by emotion, we have the opportunity to develop less reactivity and harshness towards ourselves, and maybe we could begin to grow up.

If any member struggles too greatly with this they can be allowed to simply sit and rest and let the mind go where it will. It is important however that all are present for this, and even in the event that a member finds it difficult to be still, they cannot choose to enter the room only when this piece is concluded, but must participate or be present for all aspects.

In the long term, becoming more familiar with and habituated to meditation allows for the creation of space internally. Greater ability to pause and take stock and less reactivity enters the mind stream in a broader way over time. Awareness increases: awareness of one's thoughts and feelings, of how these manifest physically to our benefit or detriment. Awareness allows choice and presents options in behaviours rather than habitual responses. One member described how he had vividly felt the impact of the meditations at around ten sessions in. This man described how a friend had made a remark that was provocative to him and which he usually tried to ignore but would end up holding significant negative feeling in the aftermath. He said that he noticed how he felt in his body and tracked his pounding heart and tight fists. He noticed how his throat closed up as if to keep in what he really wanted to say. He realised, with his increased awareness, that he now had a choice and was tired of how this person was making him feel and of saying nothing about it. He chose to speak and voice his dissatisfaction, which he had been fearful of doing as his emotion had felt too strong to be trusted. When he broke down his reactions he found this felt less powerful and he had more choice in his own reaction. He noticed the degree to which he felt calm physically after speaking and that he did not carry any feeling around with him afterwards, as would have typically been the case. He felt that as a consequence of this interaction, his self-esteem increased, as did his friend's respect for him. He said that he felt this was explicitly related to the awareness he had gained in meditation and acknowledged the value of this practice in his life.

Check In

Post meditation, it is advisable to check in with all members of the group. This can be brief and general or it can set the tone and topic for the session, depending on what members bring. Some sessions will be characterised by a few moments check in by all and a swift enough forward momentum to the theme of the session as presented by the therapists. At other times, certain members may have had significant occurrences such as bereavement, separation, serious illness of themselves or a loved one, a job loss or any other strong or seismic event.

In these cases it would be insensitive to simply plough on with a set theme in the face of such personal rupture. It is best here if the therapist acknowledges what has occurred and states that they will return to this once the whole group has checked in. Therapists can illustrate flexibility and accommodation for these particular circumstances by allowing the theme to thus arise organically from the group matrix. It is important that this is so as there is a risk of mirroring the insensitivity and minimising trauma that may be reminiscent of how the news of their abuse was met as a child, or indeed can still be met as an adult. The group at these times generally illustrates a desire to hear and support the afflicted member or members and are content to use the group time in this way. What arises here will typically apply to one of the set themes although perhaps ahead of time. The skilled therapist can make the links from the personal story to the broader themes as they would have done in any case when examining that particular theme. They can also note that one member's story or experience will likely have resonance for all participants and that this resonance can be tracked and worked with in this session. This creates sense and meaning for all regardless of who is speaking or what is to the forefront of the session.

At other times, there can appear to be a cluster of similar themes presenting at the check in. This may be self-evident or require a little more creative weaving on the part of the therapist. Sometimes seemingly disparate issues do indeed have a common thread or threads and the adept therapist is skilled in bringing these to light and providing an environment where meaning can be made of those threads. This can allow for a very organic discussion of some of the planned themes that arise within the group's own timing and with their own particular flavour. It is always wise to follow this organic material as there is often wisdom that is ripe for the mining in these seemingly coincidental overlaps. I have experienced at times an almost eerie synchronicity to these presentations and have been struck by the extent to which the timing has facilitated clients' ability to journey authentically through these pieces of work.

Once the theme has been arrived at, whether from the therapists' introduction or from the floor, the business of the group is at hand.

Group Process

Themes are identified and explored as outlined in the session chapters. A general introduction to the theme by the therapists is followed by asking members to reflect on the questions that correspond to it. These questions serve as helpful prompts to initiate the conversation and bring it along at any points where it feels stuck. They do not have to be approached in a rote fashion and will, in any case, have a good degree of overlap. It is best if therapists read the chapter related to the theme they intend to work with so as to locate themselves in the territory that will be up for investigation. It is useful for co-therapists to read and have some discussion between themselves as to their own thoughts and feelings on the theme at hand. This helps to formulate an approach and can make plain any hidden biases

Session Structure 39

or assumptions that may affect the course of the session. It is good for therapists to note what they believe may emerge for whom, to track difference and similarity between group members and to discern, in advance, anything in anyone's story that might be provocative for a fellow member. These matters can be negotiated more smoothly if they do not arise as a surprise.

While there is no pressure on every member to speak, it is good for the therapist to encourage that they do. The topics discussed can be provocative and those who speak to them in the session are more likely to move through their processing effectively. Those who do not speak can carry feeling with intensity through the week and find that this intensity only abates once they have addressed or spoken their own thoughts and feelings. It is important to say that this intensity is not negative per se – indeed it may be crucial at times and instrumental in bringing something to the boil. Every person's timing is uniquely their own and is to be respected as such. Gentle curiosity and asking questions of members is perfectly fine but if someone is clear about not wishing to speak, this should be permissible and respected. It should also be tracked with kind curiosity and followed up in the following sessions, either by the therapists or, preferably, by fellow members.

Members should be encouraged to venture their thoughts and feelings to one another. Once this is done in a respectful manner, as per the contract, risks can be taken to disagree or take an alternative perspective. The therapists should seek to encourage a movement from a more parental sensibility, where the therapists are principally looked to for guidance or affirmation, to a culture where all of the group members function as one another's co-therapists. As Jarlath Benson puts it in *Working More Creatively with Groups*, "Insist on a communal approach to work, teambuilding, problem solving" (Benson, 1987). This occurs over time and as a consequence of a build-up of trust and familiarity. Group members have been assembled on the basis of sufficient similarity and ability for insight. They are ably equipped with useful information, experiences and assistance for one another. This is both the aim and the function of the group, to create a sense of community, inclusion and understanding that can tolerate the injuries and injustices of the past. This allows unexpressed truths to be witnessed and acknowledged which in turn liberates clients from a continuing fight for this acknowledgement.

Check Out

At the close of each session, five minutes approximately before the end, a check out is an effective way of putting a boundary on the group work. This check out invites members to briefly say how they found the session and to note if it has given rise to anything that may need to be pursued further in the following session. This allows members to register any lingering unease, if it exists, and to hold this safely in a boundaried way. Members can know that even if they have not had adequate time to address provocative feelings that have arisen for them

40 Session Structure

that this has been noted and will be picked up again. Containment is modelled for participants, as is confidence that this is achievable. Each participant can reflect briefly on how the session went and note if it has brought anything up for them.

It is the goal of the group that strong emotion can be carried over into the following session, however occasionally this is not possible and significant distress or an issue of risk will require intervention after the session or prior to the next meeting. It is important that any external contact is brought back into the group and can be addressed as this prevents splitting and the apparent forming of alliances between therapists and a particular client. As the splitting may replicate old family patterns of "favourites" or "special ones", it is advisable to avoid anything that may fall into this category. One of the principal aims of the group environment is to rewrite or undo these dysfunctional family patterns by modelling an alternative way of expressing oneself within a group. As such, transparency is fundamental.

The order of the sessions, as presented, is a good general guide to the likely flow of the emergence of themes. I would recommend that the first four chapter sequences be adhered to as they lend a good foundation to the establishing of trust and a gentle way into building relationships and speaking in public. I would also recommend that the inner child piece of work be placed at session 15 to 20, as this piece needs members to be comfortable with one another and also time on the other side of it to allow for processing of what it brings to light. I would recommend that the topic of endings be raised at the halfway point to allow plenty of time for consideration of how this group might make their ending meaningful. This placing also serves to sharpen focus and remind participants that the group will end and that they should consider what they wish to achieve before the group comes to a close. It is a good interval to check if the group is giving them what they wanted or expected and to prioritise for themselves whatever feels necessary.

It is perfectly fine for the therapist to follow in rote order the chapters and themes as presented, as this works well. It may help provide a sense of structure and give a workable scaffold to the less experienced therapist. My own work with this model leaves room for these themes to emerge organically from the sessions, which will happen naturally if the therapist steps out of the way of the group process. A good degree of flexibility is beneficial when dealing with themes that will necessarily overlap and interlace. The overlaps can be noted and made apparent as a function of the educational aspect of this work. To the therapist taking the risk to run with this I would say to relax, trust your skills, trust your clients, reflect with your colleagues and work with a supervisor who has experience of working with groups.

References

Benson, J.F. (1987) *Working More Creatively with Groups*. London: Routledge.
Chodron, P. (2005) *Start Where You Are*. London: Element.
Tolle, E. (2005) *The Power of Now*. London: Hodder.

Part 4

Session Themes

Chapter 8

Introductory Session

Confidentiality Contract and Codes of Behaviour, Safe Place Visualisation, Art Piece and Discussion

Introduction

The first session is the point of origin for the group as an entity in a tangible form. It is characterised by heightened anxiety and each participant brings a healthy dose of fear through the door with them when first arriving for this brave journey. To better understand the nervousness that is in the air it is important to feel into this moment from the clients' vantage point. A shameful secret, that has been hidden from the world at large, is about to be de facto revealed, and to a group of strangers. If the community from which the population is drawn is a rural or close knit one, there is the added concern that another participant may be recognised, and for each client to be recognised in turn. It is also a hallmark of the group experience that there is a strong echo of the primary group that clients have experienced, namely the family. As families have frequently been the ground of abuse for this client group, to take this risk is great indeed and a genuine appreciation of the vividness of the anxieties needs to be front and centre for the therapist.

It is a testament to the powers of persuasion of the therapist that any client attends at all given these elements of risk, and as a consequence it is of real importance that the therapist delivers on their sales pitch and holds the group and their accompanying anxiety with assurance, skill and care. The note of welcome is thus an important one. It is beneficial to welcome the group members with tea, coffee and a biscuit as this strikes a note of familiarity and creates a routine that is customary and which helps to discharge some of the intensity of the moment. It also offsets the seriousness of the endeavour with the message that life is going on as normal and that the group is sufficiently robust to manage what is to come. To have the members sit in the circle, waiting with no distractions and an air of silence might be overly intense for what is already an anxious situation. Also, it is a small kindness, an act of nurturance and care for a client population who typically have not been met in this fashion in the world.

Once everyone has arrived and is seated the lead therapist begins with a formal welcome to the group and a restating of the group purpose and hoped for outcomes. The lead therapist outlines the plan for the session that day and invites all participants to introduce themselves by their first name and to say a little bit about how

DOI: 10.4324/9781003268888-13

they are feeling at the moment and what they would like to see changed in themselves by the conclusion of the group. The therapists open this segment by stating their own feelings and desires for the endeavour, thereby setting the tone and getting the ball rolling. In general, clients comment on their anxieties, both real and imagined, and identify feelings of shame, isolation, low self-esteem or difference that they would like to shift through engagement in the group process. It is useful for the therapist to reassure the members that their focus is indeed what the group has been gathered to address and that they are on target already.

Confidentiality Contract

Following this general introduction (in which all members will have spoken in the group and begun their participation and investment), establishing the rules of confidentiality and the guidelines for boundaries and styles of communication within the group is the next important step. The confidentiality contract (see Appendix 5) is reviewed by all members and signed off on by the close of this discussion. The contract is helpful in establishing both clarity regarding boundaries and the tone of the group, which it is crucial to set out early and name as one of tolerance and respect. This provides a "Psychological skin" for the group (Benson, 2019) that is healthy, fair and containing. Often clients' experience of group or family culture has been one of either outright or subtle disrespect, wherein their needs, feelings and experiences were not valued or regarded. It is of great importance that this theme is addressed in principal from the outset and that a clear and respectful foundation is agreed upon. It is essential that all members agree to be punctual, sober, non-judgemental, maintain confidentiality and be respectful in both their listening to others and their contributions to others. It is also important that socialisation does not occur outside the group for the duration of the therapeutic process. The therapist should take the time to explain why this is so to the group, framing this as a method of maintaining a clear boundary and minimising any risk of the therapeutic space becoming "contaminated" with any agenda other than the ones at hand. It can be suggested, even at this point, that this is open to renegotiation upon the conclusion of the group.

It is a helpful tool in a number of ways, as initial conversation is generated on some topics. There is generally some discussion required on what is to be agreed in the case of members meeting accidentally outside the therapeutic space. This is an area where there may not necessarily be consensus, with some people being content to be greeted and others not. It is worth taking time to establish what suits everyone best and allowing for individual responses and requests to be accommodated. In general, members agree to be greeted but not to engage further. It is generally acceptable to most members to be greeted if in the company of another person, but not to reveal to that third party how that individual is known to them. Most members felt comfortable to offer a generic reason to the third party, however if this is not the case for all members, there should be no difficulty accommodating this and amendments can be made as required to the contract. This makes the contract a living thing, discussed and agreed upon by all participants. The "live" nature of the contract facilitates a more genuine sense of safety and engagement than would agreeing to a set list of rules.

Safe Place Visualisation

The safe place visualisation is advantageous to members in a couple of ways. It allows members to begin the process of participating in relaxation exercises within the shared space. This lets people land, in a deeper way, into the shared space and have an experience of letting their guard down to some extent whilst in one another's company. It is the least threatening way to begin to facilitate the beginnings of feelings of safety within the group. The reason for doing a safe place visualisation at this stage is to help clients to identify imagery, of either a real or imagined setting, which is holding, peaceful and nurturing. There is sufficient choice and ambiguity within this visualisation for participants to conjure up internal or external spaces and for these to be either peopled or solitary. Prior to beginning the visualisation, it is helpful to create a space where it is possible to achieve maximum relaxation. This requires some attention to posture (it is best to be symmetrical in the body position and to have the spine straight to allow the unobstructed passage of air through the body). It is good to have blankets and pillows on hand as the body often cools down considerably during deep relaxation. It is preferable to commence with a brief physical relaxation prior to starting the exercise (see visualisation in Appendix 1).

Art Work

It is preferable to move directly into the art piece without too much conversation. As Marian Liebman notes in *Art Therapy for Groups*, "Art can be another important avenue for communication and expression, especially when words fail" (Liebman, 1997, p.2). This allows participants to remain with the sense of their safe place and to capture or describe it more faithfully. It is necessary to have a variety of media available for clients to choose from: paint, chalk, collage and clay are all good materials. There is a shift in mood and energy as members re-enter a more child-like manner of engagement, often getting down on hands and knees. Pouring paint and cutting out images is reminiscent of childhood play and it facilitates fledgling communication between members, as they reach for materials and negotiate their space and the silliness of the exercise. Allow 15 minutes for this and give a five and a three minute warning to the finishing up time.

Discussion about the Safe Place

Participants are invited to share their work by laying it out on the floor for the other members to see and discuss what their images of a safe place were. This should be done in a turn-taking manner with each participant taking roughly the same time to speak about their piece. Responses can range from a general appreciation of elements of nature, a beach or meadow setting, to more personal internal settings such as a favourite room or being in the company of a person or animal that provided a sense of security or nurture. It can be more emotive than expected, as memories of lost loved ones can be conjured, and even the connection of "safe" individuals to an unsafe time can bring up strong feelings. It is good to anticipate this and allow some time to process these pieces.

Check Out and Close

The session concludes with a check out to determine everyone's brief feedback of how they experienced this first session and to ensure that everyone is sufficiently ok to return to the next week's session. Time is usually tight at this time so if anything weighty emerges at this point, it is a good exercise to ask if the group or the individual can tolerate holding it until the next session and note that you will begin the session there next time. If it is necessary for any member to have extra time with the therapist after the group to briefly process some piece, it is important that the therapist leaves time to accommodate this, although it should not be a regular occurrence and all material should be encouraged to be brought into the group setting.

References

Benson. J.F. (2019) From training "On working with groups". Drogheda, Ireland, March.
Liebman, M. (1997) *Art Therapy for Groups*. London: Routledge.

Chapter 9

Self-Soothing

The session asks people to publicly identify the ways in which they behave and to discriminate between methods that are healthy and those that are not. We frame the work by asking participants how they mind themselves and what are the positive things they do for themselves when they are stressed or in difficulty. These often include things like going for a walk, engaging with nature, cooking, speaking to a close friend, painting or writing, sport or physical exertion. We then move to the less helpful go-tos which often include alcohol or drugs, overindulgence in food, switching off or spacing out to TV, games, virtual worlds (which may include sexual content or not) and shopping. It is not to be overly punitive or judgemental in reviewing these fixes but rather to lay them out, neutrally, and then look at them honestly. The question of degree is a pertinent one when considering benefit. Harmless escapism is often fair enough and does no damage and allows space to breathe. When the escapism or diversion takes on energy or will of its own, we may be in trouble. There is usually a clear breakdown between healthier pursuits involving a creative, nurturing or measurably positive quality with the less healthy pursuits being characterised by a measure of overindulgence or flatness in one way or another.

It's not hard to have people identify where they are with these things and most people will have a mixture of both. The ensuing conversation gently allows people to open up about some of their foibles and to experience that they are not judged and rejected for not being perfect. There is often a measure of humour in this session, which is to be encouraged as it oils the wheels of further openness and forges a sense of community.

This session aims to locate participants within the territory of themselves and from this knowledge of their own territory, to be well equipped to map and negotiate it. Self-knowledge and self-awareness are the keys to the kingdom and the aim here is to identify the default habits, routines and defences that are either helping or hindering us. This session is placed early in the programme so as to help members identify those methods of self-care that are useful and healthy as well as those that are less so. This awareness provides instant mental access to ways of nurture and support when the group material creates feelings of discomfort, grief, anger or confusion. It also sews the seed of doubt about habits or defences

DOI: 10.4324/9781003268888-14

that have a destructive root and begins the work of gently holding up the mirror to ourselves. Here, we are acknowledging positive and negative aspects as generally occurring in one bundle and normalising from the outset that this is the case for most of us. In this way we can set a tone of dispensing with judgement.

Questions for the Session

1 In what ways do you manage stress?
2 Are some of these ways more helpful than others?
3 What have you found most useful in the long term?
4 What is not so useful and why do we still do it?
5 What is it like to share this information about yourself?

Example

Participants have spoken about many methods of self-soothing over the course of the various groups. One person was sufficiently brave to begin the conversation by illustrating how physical exercise was an outlet for her and received positive soundings from the group. She could have stopped there and remained safe, but she took the risk to go further and share that this positive aspect could also have a more negative presentation and develop a punitive or compulsive aspect that was actually exhausting for her. This allowed the group to open up and all other members felt permission to identify where their own strategies could dip over into a darker aspect. This allowed for an illuminating and clarifying discussion about how much is enough and the experience of addictive tendencies and appetites. It is important to encourage members to take these risks, even in the early stages, so as to cultivate a culture of honesty and understanding.

Chapter 10

Boundaries

Placing a conversation about boundaries at this early juncture in the forming of the group is imperative. This allows a gentle and broad opening up of the conversation topic and the beginnings of disclosing personal experience as well as working out the art of conversation itself.

A launch into how participants recognise or fail to recognise their physical and emotional boundaries begins a shared exploration of the self in the context and company of the group. Members are free to go as lightly or deeply as they wish. It is helpful to distinguish between physical and emotional boundaries and to guide the conversation accordingly. There will, of course, be overlap, as all physical boundary breaking automatically breaks emotional boundary, however for the purposes of drawing out the distinctions and the commonalities, it is best to separate the categories to begin with.

Physical Boundaries

The breaking or overstepping of a physical boundary is something that is often more immediately tangible and observable, and as such is the most direct entry point to exploring this topic. Most individuals have a felt sense of how comfortable they are with physical proximity and how this differs corresponding to who the "other" in question is. It is likely to elicit some humorous responses or stories as most people have a memory of physical boundaries being breached in a social situation or of having to endure "huggers" when they are not. This laughter often lightens up the group atmosphere which is then able to proceed into more difficult territory of having encountered experiences of uninvited proximity that were felt to be creepy or discomforting. This experience of having boundaries breached in a more conscious or intentional manner is likely to be a common one in the group. As most participants will have experienced physical and/or sexual abuse, this boundary crossing is why they are attending the group in the first place.

It is common for group members to recall a "creepy" relative, family friend or boss as having offended here and to describe that they felt "unnerved" by those encounters. It is useful to track with the group how they responded to these events physically and to uncover what is typical in response to this breach of one's person.

DOI: 10.4324/9781003268888-15

Common reactions include freezing or feeling paralysed, spacing out, feeling faint or dizzy, feeling a sense of unreality, possible blindness or deafness in the moment of shock. It is helpful to ask if there was another, more visceral response that they had and that they repressed, either at the time of the event or afterwards.

The question of whether members registered these breaches of boundary with any other person is also an important one. At times the incident is witnessed by another or others and ignored or minimised. This may appear to be a passive response but it is in fact an active one, and actively discourages the victim from speaking out or acting due to the tacit message to remain silent present in the lack of objection from them. Others may have spoken and had the same experience of minimisation or direct denial. Participants may have been met with disbelief, abhorrence, rejection or anger and rage at the complainant. Even for those who were believed there was often the experience of being faced with an impotent and helpless response, tinged with shame and fear. None of these responses in any way facilitates the correct identification and management of this experience and it is sadly very common for the victim to make no further attempt to speak of their difficulty for fear of eliciting this reaction again and isolating themselves further from their communities of friends and family.

It is important to note that there may be participants who are currently in situations of ongoing physical abuse or domestic violence. These members may have further shame in speaking about this if it is assumed that this is a retrospective matter and one that should have been resolved by now. Cultivating a climate of non-judgement in relation to issues that are ongoing should be embedded into the culture of the group. This is done by direct reference to the fact that no one is perfect or has everything resolved at any juncture in their life and that change and healing are an ever expanding arc.

Emotional Boundaries

This territory will have already have begun to open up by virtue of what has already been discussed but this can be further explored by examining participants' recognition of their own emotional boundaries. Do they even know what is meant by this? It can be helpful to provide illustration here as the breaching of emotional boundaries can, at times, be more subtle than physical manifestations. Can members identify times when their needs were deliberately not met or acknowledged or their wishes were ignored? While physical abuse is instantly tangible, the menu of possibilities with emotional abuse is vast and it can be confusing for victims of this to be certain that they have experienced a transgression.

Members may identify a spectrum of experiences ranging from an ongoing scenario that they are currently struggling with to a sense of a repeating theme with many different protagonists. This may be current or retrospective but it is highly likely that most members will be struggling still to emerge from patterns of damaging relationships that carry the hallmarks of bullying behaviour and consistent disrespect. The group should explore when or if they have felt:

1   bullied
2   patronised
3   ignored or marginalised
4   verbally abused
5   dominated or controlled.

This is a rich and plentiful topic that all members will be able to readily respond to. They are also afforded here an opportunity to re-affirm their commitment to the group culture and to not re-perpetuating these behaviours or styles of engagement. This adds a dimension of safety and more robustly establishes the ground rules for engagement and exploration. This topic may easily occupy two to three sessions and it is a fundamental understanding of what needs to be grasped before moving forward.

Questions for the Session

1   How have your physical and emotional boundaries been breached?
2   How do you respond to this?
    a   Typically or
    b   Ideally?
3   Have you changed over time in your responses to having your boundaries breached?
4   What is the relationship between boundaries and respect?

Example

Laura told of how her husband was frequently derogatory towards her in his style of speech. She described how he would be critical of her appearance, actions and choices and simply of her in general. This was clearly very difficult for her to speak about, as it was a current situation. In previous sessions Laura had heard other members relate how they had endured abusive relationships and detail the process by which they emerged from these damaging dynamics. She said that it had been very jarring initially for her to hear these stories but that this had helped her to acknowledge what she knew "inside herself". With the support of the group she was gently questioned on how this made her feel and she came to realise the extent of her unhappiness in this situation. By the close of the group Laura had separated from her husband and felt very empowered regarding this choice. She was notably altered in terms of her physical appearance and had changed her manner of dressing and her hairstyle. She noted that she felt more confident and that she had been approached for a promotion at work whereas she had previously felt bypassed or overlooked. Tangible change is often an outcome of support that is consistent and compassionate, and it is not uncommon for such changes to occur in the context of the group's work and time together.

Chapter 11

Trust and Intimacy

It is a natural movement to progress from a consideration of feelings and experiences of transgression and unsafety to an examination of the qualities and characteristics of those people and situations that inspire trust and intimacy. Safety is the basis of feeling trust and trust is the basis of developing intimacy in relationship.

This session closely examines what creates a climate of feeling safe and providing a matrix for trust. Members' experiences of where and how they felt this can be recounted and mined for these qualities to be distilled and laid plain. Hallmarks of creating safety are:

1   clear communication
2   kindness
3   thoughtfulness/consideration
4   respectful behaviour
5   consistency in all of the above
6   absence of verbal abuse/gaslighting/physical abuse
7   a felt sense of equality
8   fairness or justice.

When these items are laid bare and distilled into their essence, a sharper awareness is created about what is and is not acceptable behaviour. The clarity of these norms, as well as their being named and established in the context of the group, typically gives members a greater robustness in holding, honouring and insisting on these values in their relationships. It has often been said in groups that not only was there a more instantaneous recognition of breaches of boundary, but also a far more unequivocal response of not tolerating it. This has often been said to have been facilitated by "having the group mind present" and hearing what others in the room might say. Participants have frequently noted that this sense of their fellow group members significantly helped them to hold their ground in situations of conflict, fear or difficulty, as they did not feel alone in their opinions.

DOI: 10.4324/9781003268888-16

Questions for the Session

1 What relationships have you felt secure in?
2 Why do you think these relationships felt positive?
3 What are the characteristics of a person you trust?
4 How might you develop trusting friendships/relationships in your life now?

Example

Bob described his relationship with his grandmother as having been one of the only relationships he had as a child, which was characterised by a feeling of trust and safety. He described how he yearned for visits to her house when he was not there and compared this to the chaos and violence he regularly witnessed in his own home with his parents. He spoke very movingly of the extent to which this relationship helped him to survive and to experience loving feelings, which he had always felt to be more in tune with his true nature. He commented that he is not sure that he would have been able to access those feelings within himself and may have shut them off in order to survive if not for this one pivotal relationship.

Chapter 12

Self-Assertion / Speaking
Your Truth

How, after a lifetime of keeping silent, of holding back, does one begin to speak? How do we get ourselves out of the many situations and relationship difficulties that have their origin in tolerance of and putting up with behaviours or situations that we honestly have not liked? It can seem like a minefield and indeed, it might be one. Our personal style of engagement is a part of our signature and tends to hold steady over time and circumstance. For clients who have lived through abusive situations that were ongoing, survival would have been uppermost in their schema. Living from a place of survival will require considerable damage limitation, having an eye for danger and developing the skills to avoid or minimise it. Speaking out or standing up for oneself or others would not serve you well in this context.

If self-assertion was a likely risk to incur greater violence, chaos or danger, then it would be important to learn how to squash the impulse to speak from a place of honesty or to seek to restore a sense of justice. Anger would have to be subverted and held prisoner beneath the skin and choked in the throat. This learning can have a lifelong impact and any future situation that invokes a feeling of threat, annoyance or injustice can end up being reacted to similarly. From this early place of terror in the face of confrontation, it can be difficult to emerge. The physical and emotional sensation of fear can be so overwhelming that all legitimate and reasonable forthright expression of displeasure does not occur. Indeed, it can feel as though it cannot occur.

Examining these early experiences and how clients learned to manage the unwieldy behaviour of others is important here. Many people will not make the link between how they had to act in the past, when they were in a position of powerlessness as a child, to how they feel they must act now. Drawing out the understanding of those mechanisms and of their necessity for survival as a child, and understanding that they are no longer powerless or in the place of the frightened child, is the work of this session or sessions. Once there is a realisation that this is the case, it is possible to look at alternative strategies for communicating our wishes and being clear on what we feel transgresses those wishes.

Central to making progress here is the notion of self-worth. If we do not believe that our voice or opinion have any validity, we are not likely to take any risks by

DOI: 10.4324/9781003268888-17

Self-Assertion / Speaking Your Truth   55

declaring them. Revisiting those early experiences where one's voice was not valued and acknowledging that this was wrong and an injustice are essential. This goes some way to clearing out the old position and re-establishing a more centrally located gut sense of right and wrong. Participants can at times feel defensive around the negative behaviour of others, particularly family, and excuse or minimise their actions and the impact of these. It is not uncommon to hear clients remark that controlling or intolerant behaviour reflected the attitudes or culture of the time, and to thereby let the offenders "off the hook". While this may indeed be so, it is not helpful to overlook whatever one's personal, honest response was to this and to move past a hindering sense of family loyalty that will continue to block a more authentic self-acknowledgement and expression.

Finding examples of situations that require some attention in terms of self-assertion is a great way of working this topic through. Most group members can readily identify conversations that they "have in their heads" with certain others. It can be a very amusing session as participants feel the relief of saying the unsayable in the group context and feel the support of their point of view by others. At times it can help some members refine how they may wish to speak and make more effective what might have been an overly blunt message. Finding ways to language displeasure and name a boundary are the tasks of this piece of work. Humour is a great ally here as is the occasional piece of uncensored language or "fantasy comeback" – it enlivens the session and helps see off the tyranny of fear that has silenced honesty.

It can also be one of the most difficult sessions for some as they find that they are located in marriages or family or work engagements that it would take considerable time and energy to confront and from which they may or may not emerge feeling intact. There may be genuine concerns for safety in making changes with those who would respond aggressively to it. This session can raise the issue of separation or divorce, the discomfort of caring for an abusive elderly parent or relative or the need to seek new employment. It potentially strikes at the heart of real change and can prompt perhaps long overdue but disruptive action.

Questions for the Session

1   How do you react to situations where there is disagreement?
2   What arises inside you when there is a situation of conflict?
3   How do you typically respond: a. Externally or b. Internally?
4   If these are different, why?
5   How would you ideally like to manage these instances?

Example

Sean worked with a colleague he found to be difficult. Sean told the group how this woman typically spoke to him and to some others, with a tone of condescension, and appeared to adopt a dominating manner of behaviour with him.

Sean found this provocative, particularly as he was more senior in his workplace than her. He provided the group with a number of humorous illustrations of his encounters with this lady and imagined what he would really like to say, however inappropriate. Sean received good support from the group who were highly amused and incredulous at some of the interactions. Other members suggested fitting responses to particular recurring themes of engagement and Sean felt that he had a "script" of what to say and do to best manage his colleague. He told the group subsequently that he had followed their advice and found he was much "cooler" in negotiating with this person and less rattled by his own annoyance. He said that he noticed this colleague to be unsettled by the changes he had made and felt that he had asserted himself with a minimum of drama and achieved a strong result.

Chapter 13

The Family of Origin

The family is the hub of all childhood experience. It is the matrix in which everything occurs to the child and is, in effect, its world. As such, it is difficult to overstate its influence and relevance for this client group. I have only encountered a handful of instances where the client's family was wholly innocent or naïve about the occurrence of abuse to one or more of its members. I have even more seldom encountered families where this lack of awareness was embedded in a generally loving and supportive environment, although it is important to note that this does occur. More often it has been the case that a lack of awareness regarding abuse reflected neglect, disinterest or aggression towards the children of the family. This neglect may occur as a consequence of overwhelm within the family system or it may arise out of a lack of love and nurturance in the family culture. At times it seems to stem from a felt sense of hatred or dislike for a particular child or children.

It is true that, as Jarlath Benson says, "The client comes into the room accompanied by their whole family" (Benson, 2019). This can feel palpably true in group settings, where participants frequently speak of their family experience, often before this topic is formally put on the table. It can feel as if the family is desperate to push its way into the room and be seen, which makes sense, as it is the principal point of reference for clients and the very one that needs to be examined and reset. For the therapists, there is often the necessity to "put the family back in their box" until the group comes to this piece of work. This tension is useful in helping the clients to first locate themselves in the room with their colleagues in this endeavour, before establishing how they have typically been seen and treated. This can allow the group to reflect on the gaps and differences they perceive in how they are experienced by fellow members and their families' perceptions of them.

It is natural for group members to begin mentioning their families from the start, as they are entering another family of sorts in engaging in group therapy. The group setting evokes the family for everyone and the ghosts of old positions and dynamics are inherently present. Generally these positions have not been healthy or useful for members and this new family offers an opportunity to re-cast those elements in a conscious, considered and empowering way.

DOI: 10.4324/9781003268888-18

It can be useful to look at the family in segments initially, as opposed to a functioning whole, as this can be overwhelming. I have found it useful to examine mother, father and siblings separately, although there will inevitably be overlap and reference to the wider group. Extended family can be looked at separately again, as often grandparents feature in a child's life as can aunts and uncles and cousins. The difference in the roles of mothers, fathers and siblings benefit from separating these out and looking at each individually.

Parents

It is helpful to look at mothers and fathers separately, although there will often be overlap between the two as they frequently, though not always, function as a unit where each facilitates the actions of the other. This may be done willingly or unwillingly and parents may be in cahoots or at odds, but if the parents remain together there is a tacit sense of each facilitating the other, whether that is done as a consequence of oppression and fear or from co-dependency.

I have encountered warm healthy family structures in the course of this work, where the parents were loving and certainly did their best. At times these parents were simply overburdened with large numbers of children and did not have the opportunity to be as watchful as they might otherwise have been. At other times the parents lived in a time and place where culturally they had little control or right of reply over the religious institutions that held power and that were often the source of the abuse. Other parents remained unaware of what was occurring simply because they had no exposure to acts of abuse and no reference point from which to suspect or even acknowledge the existence of such occurrences. They simply would not have held the concept or known the language and so could not have begun to address it. I recall one client whose parents were genuinely unaware of his abuse at the time that it was occurring. They played host to the parish priest, who subjected this man to ongoing sexual abuse as a boy, and at no point had any inkling that anything of the kind was taking place. The client reflected that they would have felt honoured to be so well attended by the local priest as this would have conferred status on the family within the community. Thus the client had suffered severe anxiety as a child and his parents were concerned and sought advice from their local doctor and clearly engaged with the difficulty and sought to resolve it. They were perplexed by his constant worry and his behaviour but had no idea where it was stemming from as he had never told them. When this client told his parents what had occurred as an adult they were horrified and guilt ridden that they had not known and had been so friendly and accommodating to this man.

This case was one of the very few I encountered where the parents seemed to have genuinely had no conception of what was occurring. More often, it is within the family matrix itself that abuse occurs. Often one or both parents are the perpetrators and the abuse can encompass sexual, physical, emotional abuse and neglect. It is not uncommon to have parents indulge in separate forms of abuse, with a father sexually abusing and a mother physically abusing.

Siblings

It is important to note that it is the parents who set the tone and culture of sibling relationships. Siblings will have their varying personalities, alliances and clashes as a standard function of family life, but it is how these are framed, interpreted and managed by the parents that will determine the health, or otherwise, of how these standard issues are played out.

Siblings are the peer group of the family and, as such, typically do not possess the same power and authority as parents. There are exceptions to this, however, where one child is designated a greater sphere of freedom to act in ways of their choosing and to impose those ways onto their siblings. This power can be granted by a parent as a result of intimidation by that child or by an allegiance with or similarity to a particular parent. Sibling relationships are complex and multi-faceted and a full understanding of this complex topic would require a book of its own. I would recommend reading some of the vast array of literature on this topic as a helpful insight into understanding the range of dynamics that are possible. For simplicity's sake, I will outline some of the most common occurrences as these will likely be the themes that emerge for participants.

Competitiveness

This is so common as to be mundane and is very well understood. In abusive family systems, however, this normative dance has the potential to be exploited and manipulated to a significant degree. It is not unusual to find that siblings are routinely played off against one another by abusive parents. I have frequently heard of families where one child is emphatically favoured over another in tangible ways and for this to occur in a consistent manner. Where this occurs there is a clear communication of the worth and value of individual children and it is almost impossible for those children, who are being artificially split, to ever find a path to having an easy relationship with one another. Many clients have expressed the deep struggle they have felt when a sibling who lived the same experience as them has a profoundly different view and interpretation of this experience. It can be incomprehensible when a sibling sides with an abusive parent and refutes reality, and this promotes a fracture in one's belief in memories that can have a deep and ongoing ripple.

Alliances

These are often predicated on perceiving the parents, relevant adults or other siblings in a similar way. It is of great solace if an ally can be located in the family matrix. This person serves to confirm one's perceptions of reality and provide a ballast of support. If there is an ally, there is the room to express one's authentic feelings and to have a colleague in devising tactics aimed at ensuring the optimum chance for survival. With a sibling who is a friend one can have laughter, shared interests and an experience of intimacy that allows love to be present, even in the midst of chaos. Clients often note how if there was just one person, a teacher, sibling, neighbour or grandparent, it was enough to hold onto some form of identity that endured and enabled them to endure in ways that may not have been possible otherwise.

Roles in the Family

The Parent / Caregiver

Many children adopt a particular role within the family structure. It is common to find eldest children assuming a higher level of responsibility than younger ones as they have been the pioneers and broken the parents in, so to speak, making a smoother pathway for those who come after. In difficult families it is not uncommon to find that children are afforded roles that it is impossible and inappropriate for their age and position to fulfil. Children in abusive families are typically found assuming adult roles and are overburdened with knowledge, tasks, confidences and situations that they cannot comprehend or reasonably respond to. Nonetheless, many of these children do their best to fill these roles and adapt to the unreasonable demands that are placed upon them. There is no context to challenge this setup and although many children do express their displeasure in what ways they can, there is often little or no acknowledgement of this and, indeed, they can be met with violent or aggressive responses should they fail to deliver what is expected of them. Many of these children effectively parent their parents, as well as younger siblings, as failure to do so would see the family unit come to a crashing halt. These children can carry the shame of the family and work hard to protect the family from judgement or scrutiny from the outside world. They do this from a sense of loyalty, a fear of exposure and a need for belonging in the only group that they feel they legitimately belong to.

The Blamed

Some children are victimised and set upon in their families, being designated the position of the lightning rod or the punching bag, they appear to be generally acknowledged as a person upon whom anyone's frustrations can be acted out with little consequence. At times, clients who felt they filled this role have questioned whether they were their named father's child and have wondered if they were the product of an affair or a previous relationship. They believe that this has marked them out as different from the other siblings and has allowed an attitude of intolerance and aggression to become acceptable currency, perhaps to placate the named father or punish the birth father. Often there is no proof of this but the feeling that it is true stubbornly remains. Other times this is not the case and the client reports that they reminded their parent of a disliked grandparent, sibling or family member. That this resemblance was beyond their control seems to have had little impact on the treatment they received. It is not uncommon for these children to have the family script on them become a self-fulfilling prophecy, and these siblings are at risk of issues with addiction and disenfranchisement.

The Golden Child

This child is the one who appears to receive the best treatment. They are let off more lightly in general and the parent or one parent in particular appears to favour them in obvious ways that are not concealed. Other siblings will be required to perform tasks or duties for this sibling or will be permitted to be mistreated or abused by them without incurring any consequences. This child is often lauded by the parent or parents as being somehow "special" whether this is as a result of an illness or disability or a shared disposition with a parent. It is arguable that this is an even more difficult spot to be in as the possibility of extracting oneself from the family system and attaining individuation is perhaps most difficult when one is being rewarded and stroked for a manipulative alliance. Some children extricate themselves from this position owing to a discomfort in seeing their siblings mistreated and an innate sense of justice that somehow prevails, but for many the rewards of seeming closeness and protection are hard to overthrow.

The Protector

It is not uncommon to hear survivors relate that they believed themselves to be saving or protecting another sibling or siblings from abuse by being abused themselves. Many survivors would not have had awareness that any other family member was being abused and framed their own experience of abuse as having a protective function. They feel that by absorbing the damaging behaviour, it will not be visited on a younger sister or brother and will spare them the pain that they are taking in their stead. This can happen as a means of trying to locate meaning or purpose in what is essentially a meaningless and cruel circumstance and of somehow keeping good alive in the world. It is often one of the most distressing things for siblings to realise that they had not provided any shielding for the younger ones and they can have a profound feeling of having failed their sibling, despite having clearly been blameless.

The Macrocosm / Societal Context

It is important to note that all families function within the larger matrix of the society in which they are embedded. Signs of abuse are typically there for all to see if only they were paying attention and were furnished with compassion for children and a lack of tolerance for any transgressions of their rights. In Native

62 Session Themes

American culture it is considered the greatest wrong of all "to breach the children's fire". This fire signifies the sacred rights, personal sovereignty and fundamental safety and protection of the child. That this fire is held intact by the community at large is viewed as central to the healthy functioning of their society (Dreamwalker, 2007).

Questions for the Session

1 What role did you occupy in your family of origin?
2 How did you feel about this?
3 What roles did your siblings have?
4 How did this impact you?
5 What was your mother's style of parenting?
6 What was your father's style of parenting?
7 What did you need that you did not receive in your family?
8 How can you provide this for yourself and for your own family now?

Example

Jane grew up in a family of five children. Her mother was violent and expressed aggression frequently towards Jane and three of her siblings. Jane said that her mother had many affairs and queried in her later life if her mother had worked as a prostitute. She recalled the shame and embarrassment she felt in seeing her mother in the company of men who were not her father and said that she often defended her mother to other adults who made unpleasant and judgmental comments. She said that one of her siblings, her older brother, was cosseted by her mother and not beaten as she and her siblings were. This brother was also abusive and aggressive to Jane and she recounted that her mother never reprimanded him for this. She said that she had initially felt extremely shameful speaking about her family and thought that this somehow reflected on her own identity. Jane worked through this perception of herself and with the support and encouragement of the group became much more clear on who she was. She removed herself from the remaining family ties that she felt were compromising and attempting to hold her in a position of shame and low worth. She noted that she felt lighter and more joyous upon leaving these relationships behind and said that she had an increment of energy and enthusiasm for her own creativity that was unknown to her.

References

Benson, J.F. (2019) From training "On working with groups". Drogheda, Ireland, March.
Dreamwalker, A. (2007) From training "Healing the self". Wicklow, Ireland, July.

Chapter 14

Dealing with Tyrants

Power and control are perhaps the most central and relevant of dynamics to explore when examining abusive behaviour. There is no abuse that does not involve an attempt to dominate and impose will upon another. This is routinely felt as a frightening and confusing energetic exchange that disempowers its victim suddenly, shockingly and shamelessly.

In most situations of an abuse of power the one who commits the abuse is invested with an authority that is seen to be superior to that of the victim. This may technically be the case or it may be felt to be the case. This may be as a consequence of age, family position or role, wealth or another form of seniority. The abuses may occur within familial, educational, religious, peer, social or working environments. For many survivors of childhood abuse, the family is the primary context for this experience. The shock of the initial transgression is due both to its unexpected nature and its apparent lack of shame, regret or consideration of the welfare of the victim. There is outrageousness in the event that is given no credence by the manner in which the abuse occurs. The denial of the abuse as being what it clearly is contributes to the subsequent confusion felt by the victim. As one client said "It's as if a bomb has gone off and exploded everything but everyone, including the bomber, walks around as if it had not just exploded".

The surreal element of this denial of experience and truth has a gagging effect in both the immediate and proceeding moments of the occurrence of an abuse, and it can be impossible to respond to something that's happening if part of you cannot believe, or does not want to believe, that it is really happening. Survivors typically describe a mental and physical paralysis at this time and it is common for many to project themselves out of their bodies for the duration of the abuse. Many describe engaging in this method in an ongoing way for abuse that is recurrent. This establishes a split between the mind and body and sets the individual up against themselves at some level, in a refusal to acknowledge, mentally, emotionally and physically, what is real. This split is not a personal choice that could have been more effectively managed, it is a defence mechanism employed in desperation and as a necessary means of survival.

This sense of the surreal and the feeling of abhorrence felt by the victim is often mirrored at a familial and societal level. This weaves a further layer of denial and

DOI: 10.4324/9781003268888-19

64 Session Themes

lack of acknowledgement around these occurrences and compounds the bizarre nature of the gap between the severity of the crime and an absence of its confirmation and delivery of justice. It is important that this theme is also drawn out as it makes plain to survivors how little possibility they had of escaping their circumstances and removes feelings of self-blame or responsibility for situations well beyond their control.

It is most helpful for the group to look closely at the dynamics of power and control. In magnifying and understanding the characteristics of those who attempt to dominate and control, there is an increased clarity regarding these experiences. As always, awareness is the single most effective key to liberation. The confusion and discordant feelings that have been accommodated over many years can be laid out and re-assembled to form a sensible and coherent whole. The subsequent splitting and minimising can then be seen, understood with kindness and eventually corralled into appropriate action.

Members are very likely to have multiple examples of this in their lives as the early life transgressions predispose them towards repeat offences due to having developed a high tolerance for enduring bullying behaviour. It is common to hear many stories of childhood and adult bullying, workplace harassment, friends who consistently take advantage, violent or controlling partners or ex-partners or even adult children of whom they are fearful.

The Dynamics of the Tyrant

- Gaslighting
- lies
- lack of empathy
- lack of love
- takes discernible pleasure in controlling / having power over
- atmosphere of fear even when nothing happening / controlling from afar
- derogatory speech
- superiority
- inability to tolerate difference of opinion / must be right
- must be obeyed
- manipulation (mental, physical or emotional)
- suicide as a threat
- lack of self-responsibility
- continuous negative projections forcefully stated or implied.

Questions for the Session

1   How do you feel in your body/mind/heart when encountering this behaviour?
2   How does this remind you of abuse you experienced as a child?
3   Does it recall dynamics present in your family of origin?

Dealing with Tyrants 65

4 What is your authentic reaction to this behaviour... if fear was not present? (body/mind/heart)
5 How could you express this safely?

Exercises

1 Draw, paint or sculpt the feeling of being dominated or oppressed.
2 Make a representation of the feeling of being liberated from this.

Example

Tom spoke about how he was having difficulty currently with a work colleague. This colleague had recently been promoted over him and had subsequently begun to exert their authority in a manner that Tom felt was exploitative. He described that he found the person's actions hard to address as they were "so bad you would have to have a fight" if he was to engage with the individual in question. He said that he feared his own anger at the person was rendering his response inadequate. He used the group space to examine how this scenario was reminiscent of how his mother had treated him and that was why he was so charged and ineffective when it came to making an appropriate response. The group helped him to identify a route of official complaint and to endorse his experiences as being unacceptable. This facilitated him to find a path of resolution through formal processes and to ultimately feel empowered in the situation. He noted that this had the effect of somehow also liberating him from an old dynamic he experienced with his mother and to go forward differently in this relationship.

Chapter 15

Anger / Rage

It is not surprising to locate a strong measure of anger in a population that has experienced abuse. Anger is an insufficient word to capture the justifiable outrage that must arise in reaction to such extreme breaches of trust. Rage is a far more appropriate word. The experience of abuse encompasses so many transgressions of the child's person and of their world, that there is a severe damage to a sense of safety and boundary that for most children is assumed and basic. A child's initial horror and shock would be quickly followed by feelings of rage in many cases, however it is not a feeling that can be fully acknowledged, or in many cases be acknowledged at all.

A child's abuser is generally well known to them and to their family, or is a parent, sibling or member of their extended family. The closeness of this relational proximity involves a dependency on or an intimate networking with the perpetrator. This closeness, coupled with a genuine difficulty in languaging a previously unheard of experience, compromises the option of expressing anger and outrage towards the relevant target. There is a common dynamic of an interplay of fear, shock, disbelief, confusion, grief and anger spinning in a loop and all the while the victim will be attempting to restore the former order and sense of goodness and rightness they would have assumed was present in the perpetrator.

In cases where the perpetrator is a parent, it is simply not possible for the child to fully acknowledge the parent's "badness" or "wrongness". The child is wholly dependent upon the parent and their own sense of identity, safety and survival is so keenly entwined with them that it is, I believe, psychologically impossible for them to locate cruelty and betrayal with their primary carers. The only alternative is to relocate that "badness" within themselves, as a means of both having some potential control and allowing the parent to remain "good". Anger, in these instances, is directed towards the self, who is believed to have done something that merited this abusive behaviour. This internal lie to the self is a psychological manoeuvre that is choiceless and is completed as a defence in the name of survival. It is the principal anger that needs to be understood, ironed out and redirected in order for healing to occur.

Some survivors of abuse have been at the end of the rage of others and have encountered this in a number of negative ways including physical violence, verbal

DOI: 10.4324/9781003268888-20

attacks, abandonment and controlling behaviour. It is a common reaction for those individuals to disassociate themselves from any identification with anger, as it is designated as a quality of the abuser. This places all feelings of anger into the shadow realm and creates a barrier to acknowledging, identifying and recognising those feelings within oneself.

A key element of the work of this session is *granting permission* for the feeling of rage and making it clear that feeling or expressing it does not affiliate them with abusers. It is important to acknowledge the universality of the minimising of this emotion, at a societal level in general and in particular as felt by victims of abuse. By drawing out the scenarios that members were captive to and more fully understanding how impossible it would have been to express rage, participants can understand how they were coerced into burying this feeling given the lack of acknowledgement and the lack of any possible means of expression.

It is useful to link this experience to the way in which participants process anger currently and for them to make links between old and present patterns. Clients may find that they struggle to assert themselves in any conflictual situation or they may identify that they are very reactive in a manner that holds too much heat or fear. Patterns and reactions that occur in the present are very likely to have strong roots in the past and in the identifying of these patterns, room is created for alternatives that can have a healthier origin and produce a more beneficial result. As Umberto Eco says in *Inventing the Enemy*, "Fire is called when something has to be changed" (Eco, 2012, p.45).

Some situations may arise where participants admit to behaviour that may warrant intervention. If any member identifies that they take their anger out on their children or on others in any way that constitutes risk or inappropriate behaviour, then this must be acknowledged and addressed.

Suggested Meditation

Relaxation followed by Anger Visualisation.

Note: This visualisation requires some preparation and explanation. Participants are to be encouraged to anticipate some discomfort and reactive feelings and the therapist must normalise this experience and reassure participants that they can manage this, even if it stretches them somewhat. It is important to remain with these feelings as opposed to repressing, denying or running away from them. It is only in remaining with this difficult material and expressing and understanding it that a fresh understanding can be reached.

Exercise

Illustrate through paint or clay how you experience the emotion of anger or rage. Share this in the group discussion.

Questions for the Session

1 How do you experience the feeling of anger? What are the sensations/thoughts/physical reactions?
2 Can you represent this visually?
3 How do you habitually react to others when you are angry? To yourself?
4 Would you like to respond differently? How?
5 Have you ever seen anger managed well?
6 How did others react to you when they were angry?

Example

Laura chose to work with clay for this exercise in visually representing her anger. This piece of art therapy followed a guided visualisation that explored the texture and experience of sitting with anger and rage. She sculpted a dragon in red clay with outstretched wings that roared with an open mouth and sharp teeth. The piece was striking and evocative and appeared most life like. When speaking about her work afterwards Laura said that she was surprised by how "good" it was as she was not a visual artist. She noted that it had emerged exactly as she had intended whereas with much other artwork this was not the case. She described that the dragon was pierced in the heart and that she had wished to convey the anguish of a combination of both sharp hurt and burning rage. She said that she felt that her sculpture had "perfectly" captured her intention and mirrored her inner experience. She noted the relief she felt in being able to "call a spade a spade" and felt that the dragon was a powerful beast that reconnected her with her own power. She subsequently went on to collect dragons, as statues or paintings or even toys, and felt this to be symbolic of her gathering power and knowing that had been previously compromised.

Reference

Eco, U. (2012) *Inventing the Enemy*. London: Vintage.

Chapter 16

Grief and Depression

Grief is an unavoidable experience for every person walking the planet. It is not possible to live a life unaffected by sadness and there are few amongst us who would profess it to be so. We are all at some time afflicted by loss, sickness or death. The Buddhist teacher Chogyam Trungpa directly addresses this truth by noting simply that "obstacles always arise" (Trungpa, 1993). To a lesser extent, we have all been acquainted with the experience of not getting our way or of having things go differently and disturbingly against the way we had wished them to go and have had to rearrange ourselves and our lives accordingly. As natural and as unavoidable as it is to feel pain, loss and sadness, we seem to hold the illogical position of being surprised and affronted by it. This creates the predicament of not only having to absorb and contain grief but of simultaneously processing shock and then judging and measuring both the difficult events and our own reactions to them. Even as I write this sentence it seems as though this is all just too much to process. One can imagine that a computer asked to download this level of material would be unable to complete the task and might well combust or overload. It is understandable how human beings, equally, deem some levels of pain and suffering to be simply "too much", and consciously or unconsciously shut down at some level. Usually this shut down is an emotional one.

Grief requires time, patience, compassion and understanding. It is not a feeling that moves through the system at any speed and is an entity that has its own time, style and way. As Clarissa Pinkola Estes says in *Women Who Run with the Wolves*, "with changes of the weather, the scar can and will ache again. That is the nature of true grief" (Estes, 1992, p.384). Grief is natural, meaning that it is endemic to the human condition and as such it is beyond the judgement of being right or wrong; it simply is. If the conditions in which someone who is experiencing grief are not understanding of that feeling, or are unkind and intolerant of it, it is a feeling that is likely to go underground. If it does not feel safe to be vulnerable (and grief and sadness in their full expression will necessitate an honest vulnerability – we cannot defend ourselves when we are on our knees) then this feeling cannot be fully met and worked through. If conditions are unfavourable the truth and the full experience of grief will be atrophied and the sufferer will likely find that some rich and valuable aspects of the self are cut off and exiled

DOI: 10.4324/9781003268888-21

70 Session Themes

alongside the pain. As Estes notes, "the keeping of secrets interferes with the natural self-healing hygiene of the psyche and spirit" (Estes 1992, p.384). If this occurs the individual is more likely to find that this unworked sadness will manifest as depression.

Loss of aspects of the self can also drive depression. The unlived life can cast a long shadow, and when people have a sense of skills, abilities or passions that they have never fully lived, this can cause a rift in the internal experience of the self. For some, their talents were devalued or denied by their family or the culture they grew up in, for others the necessary financial support was not available and a more baseline physical need for survival surpassed the time and training that would have been required for their more authentic calling. Once life has been survived physically, the sense of what might have been and of the feeling of the impossibility of re-accessing those untended dreams can drain one's enthusiasm for what remains of life.

As I have encountered depression over many years, it has always been a grief or griefs that were ultimately identifiable but had been subverted due to a lack of support. As these griefs grow more distant with time, the person loses the narrative of the origin of their sadness, which becomes less and less accessible to them. The sense of sadness becomes more globally located and all pervasive. They are left with a "ghost" feeling of dissatisfaction and lack of fulfilment, of something unresolved, that they unconsciously feel to be unresolvable, a curse or a doom that carries a feeling of dread and foreboding. Fear sneaks into the original grief and further compounds the difficulty and undesirability of reaching and understanding it.

Anger too, has its role here. I have often found it to be the case that anger and depression were two sides of the same coin. Once the anger at the lack of support and the awfulness of the loss or the harm done can be acknowledged or expressed, the grief can be more easily accessed. At other times a lengthy depression that may appear as grief actually masks an anger that requires expression. Once this anger can be accessed, a more authentic grief emerges. This grief has a healing and more finite quality that can be moved through and emerged from; it differs from a depressive fugue in that it has the shape of known stories and remembered feelings. This renders the sadness as graspable and concrete, it makes it into something that can be met and potentially understood. Understanding provides clarity and clarity provides liberation.

Questions for the Session

1　Have you experienced feelings of sadness or grief?
2　Have you felt depressed?
3　Is there a difference between these two feelings? If so what?
4　Have you overcome a loss or a feeling of sadness?
5　What helped you to overcome this?
6　Do you feel that you have unclaimed skills, passions or dreams?
7　What could you do to reclaim these?

Example

Loni spoke in the group about how there was no culture of acknowledging emotion in her family other than anger. She said that any remonstrations to her parents of sadness or unhappiness were customarily dismissed and that she was belittled as being weak and told that she "needed to toughen up". She said that this had caused her to develop an overly harsh attitude towards herself in many aspects of her life. She illustrated her high level of perfectionism in how she approached her career, physical appearance and levels of endurance, both physical and emotional. She told the group that she had volunteered for a mountain climb that she did not, in fact, think she was capable of nor wished to do. In talking this through in the group setting, Loni realised that she was "performing for an invisible audience" and decided to pull out of this venture. She chose instead to spend her time enjoying her home baking with her children, which she said she had a genuine passion for but had felt was not important enough to indulge in. With the help of the group feedback she began to embrace what actually gave her joy and to engage less with other people's measures of worth.

References

Estes, C.P. (1992) *Women Who Run with the Wolves*. London: Rider.
Trungpa, C. (1993) *Training the Mind and Cultivating Loving Kindness*. Boston, MA: Shambhala.

Chapter 17

Loneliness

Exploring this subject is a deep dive into a deep topic. Feelings of loneliness are an unavoidable aspect of being human and there is no one who escapes this feeling forever. Moments of change and growth almost necessitate a period of feeling alone and different to what is familiar so as to re-determine one's identity and recast oneself with fresh understanding. Almost all of us will outgrow persons and situations throughout our lifetime and these transition times are characterised by a measure of fear of the new and of being apart for a time until the dust settles and new opportunities appear. This is not only normal but necessary and it is helpful to guide the group in making this distinction between healthy, reflective space and a more pervasive and unproductive state of loneliness or isolation.

A more ongoing sense of being alone, different and unaccepted are often central feelings to this client group. It is one of the primary functions of this work to target this strong and often solid sense of being alone. This sense arises as a consequence of feeling that one is singular and different from others in one's difficult and taboo experiences and from having seen and felt that those experiences cannot be heard, tolerated or digested on either a familial or a societal level. This leaves those who have experienced abuse and trauma in an impossible position, where the nature of what has occurred is extreme and significant and as such requires witnessing and processing, and where, in general, there is an abhorrence of the subject matter which renders this unlikely to occur.

It is often said that there is an unspeakable quality to the experiences of abuse that mitigates the keeping of the secret of its occurrence. While there is truth to this, particularly for children, who do not have the vocabulary or conceptual frame of reference to describe their experience, it may be more accurate to say that there is an unhearable or indigestible aspect to it as well. In my experience, most survivors of abuse have indeed tried to tell someone of what was occurring. The telling may have been a relatively straightforward if fearful attempt at describing what was happening or a more veiled attempt that sought to hint or infer or act out aspects of their experience.

Many survivors recall that these attempts were rebuffed, ignored or denied outright. These denials, for they are all methods of denial, are often experienced as being as wounding as the abuse itself, sometimes even more so. It is an act of

DOI: 10.4324/9781003268888-22

recognition in itself to admit that one's attempt to tell was denied as children usually find this so painful that they will find another way to interpret it. It is common to feel that they did not explain clearly enough or that they had somehow not said what they had said. This serves to protect the "safe" adult in the child's mind. It is simply too devastating to be failed by the one they confided in as well as the one they were abused by.

The sense of being alone in the world with your suffering denied is a sharp one. The message that this is your problem and yours alone is clear, as is the shame inherent in the discreet or direct request to keep the suffering hidden and secret. All individuals know who they are by sharing and confiding and receiving feedback on their thoughts and feelings and observations. Where this is not possible there is a stark isolation and a sense of being hermetically sealed off with your shameful experience and the strong sense that you are different from others. The breaking of this seal is the work of the group.

Questions for the Session

1   How do you personally experience loneliness?
2   Is it necessary to be alone to be lonely?
3   What causes you to feel loneliness?
4   Is it your own behaviour or that of others?
5   Can you enjoy being alone at times?

Example

Shane described that he has an ongoing sense of difference from others. He described that his awareness of his history of experiencing abuse is always with him and that he feels this to have a very big presence in his mind and his subsequent sense of identity. He described how unusual it is to have such a large aspect of one's life be an unknown thing to almost everyone he knows and described it as like having a big secret. This led Shane to feel that nobody really knows him and that even close friends are not as close as they think they are. He further described that this secret feels shameful and that, in his mind, if people did know, they would cease to be as friendly with him and an awkwardness or distance would inevitably creep in. He looked in the group session at how this made his loneliness a *fait acompli* as he had already decided that sharing his past would alienate him from others rather than potentially forge a deeper intimacy. This assumption was challenged in the group and other members shared that this had not necessarily been true for them. This gave Shane the courage to take a risk outside of the session and make a different, healing and restorative experience. He felt grateful that he had been challenged and said he was beginning to feel more warmth in his connection with others.

Chapter 18

Shame

Shame is perhaps one of the most hidden aspects within the territory of sexual abuse. On an anecdotal level, this is very apparent to me socially, where mention of my work is routinely met with a hybrid of embarrassment, aversion and awkwardness on behalf of others. The conversation usually winds down quickly and I have learned to provide quick links to alternative topics to relieve the discomfort of others. If this is my experience as a supposed professional, I can only imagine the dread of survivors.

This dread is in part due to not knowing if others are clear on the realities of sexual abuse or if they harbour sympathetic or minimising views about perpetrators. The many conversations that have arisen at a societal level, from clerical abuse to the alleged sexual abuse perpetrated by sports personalities or celebrities, illustrate that a range of opinions are present. Any response from outrage on behalf of the victims to outright denial of the occurrence of abuse is possible and survivors do not know which friends and acquaintances are on which side of the fence. Every new scandal that receives media attention is a possible gateway to either the deepening or damaging of relationships.

Shame clings particularly fast to abuse that is sexual in nature. Survivors of physical violence, emotional abuse and neglect, while deeply affected and impacted by these abuses, do not seem to carry the sting of shame with quite the same intensity as survivors of sexual abuse. Other violations can be languaged more readily and at an earlier age whereas sexual abuse is harder to speak about and carries the taint of "dirtiness" and "perversion".

It is not entirely clear to me why neglect, violence and emotional abuse of a child would not be considered as perversions in exactly the same manner but it usually appears that these aspects are less hidden than abuse of a sexual nature and that shame is one of the tactics most frequently employed by perpetrators in order to vouchsafe silence. It is not unusual, as part of the grooming process, to make a child feel complicit in the abuse, either by giving treats (the acceptance of which is manipulated to imply a tacit permission for abuse to occur), showing them pornographic images, telling a child they are "special" or frightening them with the possibility of "getting in trouble" if the abuse is discovered. As Phil Mollon notes in *The Fragile Self*, "Self- consciousness arises in the jarring between

DOI: 10.4324/9781003268888-23

the collusive fitting in with the desire of the other and the actual separateness of the self" (Mollon, 1999, p.74). This self-consciousness is an acute feeling where, as Erickson observes, "One is visible and not ready to be visible" Erickson (1959, p.120). These tactics have the effect of transferring a feeling of responsibility and guilt to an innocent party. If the abuse is perpetrated by a close family member, on whom the child is dependant, this is an even more potent silencing method.

In working with this subject it is important to draw out the grooming process and make explicit the methods and devices used to bind children to secrecy and recurrence, in a conscious and deliberate manner. One of the most common questions or regrets expressed by survivors relates to the recurring nature of the abuse. People often wonder why they did not shout, object, avoid the abuser or tell anyone. It is important that group therapists are clear as to the answers why.

Why Children Don't Tell / The Grooming Process

1   Often children actually have tried to tell. Children are very adept at measuring responses or likely responses and tailoring their actions to match. Many adults who I have worked with, who initially said that they had never told anyone, on further investigation, found that they had either told and been rejected outright, or tried to tell or hinted and had this ignored or minimised. If this rejection of their suffering was by a parent, this is a further and arguably sharper trauma. The relationship with parents or carers who appear not to care can be irrevocably damaged at this juncture.

2   Some children do not speak of the abuse as their home situation is an unstable and/or dangerous one. They do not expect to be met with understanding or a protective impulse on behalf of parents or guardians and so they do not volunteer for the added trauma of having this fear confirmed.

3   Oftentimes predators choose children who are neglected in terms of attention or affection. These victims are usually lured in with attention and affection that is non-sexual in the initial stages. This provides the appearance and experience of a much-needed nurturing relationship for such a child, and as such it is overwhelmingly positive at the outset. When this "nurturance" reveals itself to have a sinister aspect the child is confused, in shock, fearful and conflicted. An aspect of nurturance that is desired and necessary for survival is mingled with an aspect to which there is a sense of aversion and the resulting feelings are confusion and conflict. The child will not want the adult to be "bad" and is more willing for the "badness" to be located within themselves than in an adult whom they perceive as more powerful and on whom they are dependant and, most crucially, who they love.

4   Perpetrators often bribe children and bind them to secrecy in this fashion. The bribes can be seductive or fear based. Seductive bribes include provision of sweets, toys, attention and non-sexual affection (which very neglected children may be desperately in need of). Use of pornography and the induced physical arousal of the child may be used as a lure given that older children

will be naturally curious regarding sexuality. This natural and healthy curiosity, which would run in parallel with the appropriate exploration of this theme in the peer group, is manipulated consciously to the perpetrator's own end. This is particularly effective in manufacturing shame and silence, as the child cannot deny the physical reactivity of their body, which will appear to them as having been complicit.

5 Some perpetrators use fear to ensure silence. It is not uncommon for threats to be made to the child's family or to suggest that the child themselves would be discredited and judged for the abuse. In situations where the perpetrator is a close family member or a parent, the threat of the loved one being sent to prison and "going away forever" is often a terrifying one, both in terms of loss of a needed adult and in terms of the weight of that kind of responsibility on a child.

In working through this topic, it is useful for each member to become clear about the grooming methods that were used on them. There is a need to dispel the myth that this situation was escapable by them if only they had acted differently or been more clever or resourceful. It is helpful to make clear the inescapability of their situation and circumstances and to absolve them from false and impossible responsibilities. This allows the guilt and shame to be squarely given back to the perpetrator, who has disowned it and placed it with them.

Questions for the Session

1 How do you define shame?
2 In what ways do you feel shame within yourself?
3 What is the physical/mental/emotional feeling of shame?
4 What do you think has caused these feelings?
5 Do these feelings have any basis in truth?
6 What is the difference between regret and shame?

Example

One participant recalled how he had been abused by his mother. He said that he experienced overwhelming shame in relation to many aspects of her behaviour as she was alcoholic and neglectful to him and his siblings. He recounted that she worked as a prostitute and described his hatred of this and his anger towards her as existing in conflict with his love for and need of her. He told how she would frighten him with the threat of her going to prison if her activities were reported or known and he feared for the survival of his siblings and himself. In tracking this in the group, he became clearer on the impossibility of this set of circumstances and of the inappropriateness of the responsibility he was given to hold. He identified a sickening feeling in his stomach and spoke of how this feeling persisted in the present and had been cause for medical investigation. As he examined this further he tracked that the feelings of nausea contained both rage and profound disappointment and he felt ill in the session. Following this tracking and subsequent awareness, he noted that the strong feelings of nausea subsided to a degree and he felt that much of his physical suffering had its origin in unprocessed emotions and that since these emotions had been brought into awareness, their power had significantly reduced. The understanding and witnessing of the group to his early life was instrumental in freeing him from the shame he carried about his mother's behaviour.

References

Erickson, E. (1959) *Identity and the Life Cycle*. New York: International Universities Press.
Mollon, P. (1999) *The Fragile Self: The Structure of Narcissistic Disturbance*. London: Whurr.

Chapter 19

Sensuality and Sexuality

Sensuality is a wonderful word. It connotes pleasure that has its roots in the physical realm as opposed to the mental. It covers a multitude and resides in all of the senses, so that taste, touch, sound, scent and sight are all potential sites of enjoyment and delight. The options of sensual enjoyment range from taking pleasure in food, warm baths, massages, children's hugs, cashmere and silk clothing, swimming in the salty sea, listening to or playing a piece of music, feeling the warm sun or smelling a favourite perfume or aroma. The possibilities are almost endless, and the joy derived is simple, pure and widely available.

The body's ability to draw pleasure from life is often compromised when the body has been violated or abused and these experiences can have the effect of alienating survivors from their bodies, as they are deemed unsafe or something of a liability. The sensual world may be viewed as a gateway to the sexual world and as such can be feared, neglected or abandoned. It is a most unjust theft and one that it is worth challenging in the context of a supportive group framework.

It is advisable to look principally at sensuality before moving to questions and considerations that relate more directly to sexual expression. In examining sensuality there is an implicit permission for the body to feel good and an equally important permission for this feeling to be claimed and celebrated. In Ireland, where I have principally practiced, for many, healthy conversation around physical and sexual issues was obstructed by a harsh religious doctrine that deemed such topics as "dirty or sinful". Open conversation or exploration of such matters was essentially taboo (a position which allowed many of those who upheld those doctrines to sexually abuse children with impunity). While this has moved on considerably and those same doctrines do not hold the same degree of power now, there is nonetheless a legacy of this climate that remains. It can still be awkward to speak frankly about matters that are common to everyone and a pall of shame and embarrassment is palpable to this day.

Commencing the discussion with the sensual affords a comfort to acknowledging that the body is alive and aware and, most importantly, not bad. Sharing around this is generally lighthearted and uplifting, members will often overlap on what they enjoy and the soil is well tended for a broader discussion that encompasses blocks, discomforts and limits. It is important to state that nothing is right

DOI: 10.4324/9781003268888-24

or wrong here, some members will have healthy functioning sex lives and others will not. Some will have an aversion to sex and sexuality that is clear and distinct and which they do not want to challenge, enjoying, as they might, a celibate life free from the pressures of such considerations. The work of the group is not to dictate what is correct or otherwise in this very varied arena, but to question what has been settled for, accepted or denied and to examine alternatives where there is dissatisfaction.

Questions for the Session

1   What does sensuality mean to you and how do you experience this?
2   Can you give an example of a sensual experience you enjoy?
3   What is your favourite sense?
4   Does sensual enjoyment ever feel negative/wrong?
5   What is the relationship between sensuality and sexuality?
6   Does sexuality feel safe?
7   How do you express your sexuality?
8   Would you like this to be different in any way? If so, how?

Example

Philomena spoke over the course of three weeks on this topic in the group. At first, she had spoken plainly and unapologetically about how she no longer had any intimate life with her partner, whom she cared about but felt no desire for. She reflected that she had never felt sexual desire and that she had only engaged in sex functionally in order to conceive her children. She said that it was a relief to her to have been clear with her partner that she would not participate in a sexual life with him and that this had removed a sense of expectation on his part. Over the course of the following weeks, she had, encouraged by listening to others in the group, discovered erotic literature. She spoke of noticing feelings of sexual desire that were entirely new to her and which had surprised her greatly. There was much humour in the session as she recounted her surprise and she was very well supported by the group in continuing to explore this new dimension of herself. She told how she had never taken pleasure in her own body before and that while she was enjoying discovering this on her own for now, she was considering opening up this area of herself with her partner. It was notable to me that the group was so well able to speak of sexuality once there was a feeling of safety, and it is fair to say that I was genuinely taken by surprise by the extent of the shift of this group member!

Chapter 20

Fear

This is a strong subject and is one of the topics that is likely to be experienced with a high level of intensity by the group. Many if not all of the participants are likely to be intimate with fear both retrospectively and, to a greater or lesser degree, currently. It is important to note that for some members fears may be a product of past events and primarily located in memories or flashbacks, and for some there may be situations or individuals who are legitimately fear inducing in the present. This can lead to this topic having a two-tiered approach where the past and the present fear experiences are distinguished and the influence of the past on the present can be more clearly drawn out.

It is useful to commence this session with a safety-based visualisation to set a grounding of protection and holding prior to exploring such a provocative theme. The candle visualisation is appropriate at this juncture.

As participants move into considering the role of fear in their own lives, they will become activated around the topic. This raises the ghost of fear, so to speak, not to intentionally frighten people, but to provide the taste of the territory they will be exploring. Therapists will ask participants to identify what situations, individuals or memories are fear provoking for them. These stories are then explored in two ways: one, to track at a physiological level what is happening in the body in the experience of fear; and two, to unearth the track ways and various manifestations of this emotion through the body, mind and emotions. There will be considerable crossover between these aspects, but it is useful to distinguish the different elements involved, which helps to focus and to dismantle an often overwhelming and "global" feeling into its constituent parts. Doing this allows fear to be experienced while it is not naturally present, which in turn allows more freedom to examine it given the distance. Fear is such an unpleasant experience that it is instinctive to most people to attempt to back away from it as quickly as possible and certainly not to look for it if it is not present. This has the effect of leaving the experience unexamined and, as a consequence, there is then little personal choice or felt alternatives when it is experienced. This counterintuitive process of looking directly at fear reverses its power to overwhelm in the moment due to a raised awareness of what is actually taking place.

DOI: 10.4324/9781003268888-25

Questions for the Session

1   What causes you fear? (memories of abuse, angry people, money worries, children, phobias etc.)
2   How do you experience this in your body/mind/emotions? (sick stomach, spacing out, headache, coldness, heat, palpitations etc.)
3   How do you react when you feel fear? (paralysis, anger, panic, run away/avoid, speed up or slow down etc.)
4   What would you like to do or feel differently?

Example

One example of such an experience was made clear by a client of one group cycle who described her relationship with her husband as being one in which he dominated and behaved with little consideration for the effect of his behaviours on others. This participant noted her fear-based reaction to his style and became aware of how she would "lie low" as a strategy of avoiding conflict with this difficult person so as not to escalate things and provoke a possible violent reaction. In the course of examining fear in the group, she tracked the similarity to her reactions in the present to those of the past and noted the similarity between the character of her father and her husband. She identified her personal style that she engaged as soon as she experienced feelings of fear and discovered a greater understanding of its origin. The group explored the specifics of how exactly she would lie low in order to shine a light on the details of this behaviour. She was able to track her body language, verbal responses and other avoidant techniques and to map how the feeling of fear presented physically in her system and to become aware of the movement of this through her physical, mental and emotional system. This awareness, once uncovered, cannot be unseen or unknown and once the repetition and familiarity of a particular cycle is exposed, it loses its power to convince in as robust a fashion. This allowed this client to bypass the automatic reactions and respond in another way, which in turn created a different response in her husband and a new dynamic was created.

It is important to say that there are times when the reasons for feelings of fear are not as solid as may be imagined by the client and there are also times when fear is the correct and appropriate state. Some of the participants may be in relationships with volatile partners who would indeed become dangerous when they are met with increased self-assertion or changed boundaries. It is important that we as therapists are not cavalier about this and that client safety is a paramount concern. There are times when this topic may bring to light situations that require safety or barring orders or necessitate the involvement of third-party agencies such as the police or child protection agencies. It is crucial that should these issues present they are not skirted around or avoided as to do so would potentially put someone in danger and cause the facilitators to lose credibility in the eyes of the group. This may require time to be allocated outside of group and if this is needed it must be followed through. It is not possible to model the strong holding required if right action is not taken in the face of situations that clearly require intervention.

Chapter 21

Suicidality

The topic of suicidality is likely to be an intimate one to a group of survivors of abuse. It is a subject that most, if not all, of the group members will have brushed up against at some point, whether that encounter is an internal or an external one, or indeed both. Many survivors have incurred abuse, in part, due to a higher than customary level of vulnerability. This vulnerability often points to a family system that is itself in jeopardy and straining under the weight of potentially multiple issues. It is not uncommon to find severe neglect, alcoholism, emotional abuse, violence or atmospheres of heightened fear. And it is not uncommon for such familial legacies to claim victims of suicide. The dearth of any lineage of coping skills, parenting or appropriate valuing of children can render these children vulnerable to suicide as adults.

The domino effect of this vulnerability and lack of being valued is an increased likelihood of making destructive relationship and life choices and repeating the pattern that has been experienced growing up. Familiarity has a strong pull, and it is notable how often elements of a survivor's marital relationship mirrors that of their parents or reflects a lack of self-worth. Survivors can find themselves stuck in a repeat of the past, with no strategies for exit or sufficient self-esteem to rally the necessary confidence and assertion to alter their circumstances. Making the journey of life may seem like an impossible request, akin to being asked to run a marathon having done no training, and it is not surprising that faced with this overwhelming sense of impossibility there are those who choose to leave the race.

Group members may have a family member or friend who has committed suicide and have been plunged into the territory of suicide unwillingly. They may have long grappled with suicidal ideation and self-harm or have those in their lives who are struggling in this way. This may be an issue that is in the past or the present and it is probable that in any group there will be a mixture of both. As with other themes that have gone before, this is a most sensitive area but one that benefits from an honest airing by a well-established group, who may indeed feel it a great relief to have permission to speak freely on the subject.

Suicides that have been experienced by group members of family, friends or others will most likely have aspects of unresolved emotion. It is such a taboo subject that it is rarely if ever handled well at a societal level and carries the tinge of

DOI: 10.4324/9781003268888-26

shame and even sin. This lack of acceptability for the act leaves those who survive it caught in the net of not knowing how to speak of it or not knowing if they are allowed to speak of it. Before coming to terms with the loss of the individual who has died, there is a wave of potential judgement (that the person is wrong, selfish or bad for having done it), horror (at the violence and/or desperation of the victim) and guilt (that they might have prevented it if they had paid greater attention or somehow acted otherwise). The complicated act of grieving is more torturous still with these additional features.

Members may struggle with the fact that they felt angry at the victim whilst they felt they should feel sad. Feelings of abandonment, confusion, hurt and even jealousy may arise. It is possible that comparison goes on internally with their own life and that of the deceased and the suicide of another may bring forward the legitimacy of one's own right to end life.

It will not be possible to resolve every aspect of this dense subject, but it is of great value to allow the conversation to happen. The chance to address this mammoth topic in a spirit of truth and non-judgement already goes a long way towards moving through its more stuck aspects. This lets disbelief and shock be witnessed and shared and allows grief to happen as it should.

Suggested Meditation

The Golden Light Visualisation (see Appendix 2, p. 112).

Questions for the Session

1 What do you feel about suicide?
2 What does it leave behind for those who survive it?
3 Why do you think someone commits suicide?
4 Do you feel it can be prevented?
5 How would you manage suicidal feelings?
6 How do you take care of yourself in the aftermath?

Example

One client spoke of a suicide in the community that was recent. The person spoke of having attended the funeral of the suicide victim and how she felt that it was a waste of the person's life and a genuine tragedy. She said that this had affected her own thoughts of self-harm and suicide and she wondered why she could feel this way about the suicide of someone other than herself and yet not experience the same compassion for herself. She felt that this line of questioning and the ability to speak openly in the group had shifted her logic and helped her to see her own value and to increasingly regard her life as precious and not to be wasted. Others joined the conversation and there was a strong sense of sadness and desperation that benefited tangibly from having the chance to be aired. By the close of the group there was a marked increase in a shared sense of compassion in the room, both for others and for oneself. This is the stuff that is hard to measure and it is only possible to rely on the reported experience of others, however it is no less real and valuable for that.

For facilitators who feel nervous about opening up this topic, it is best to have no goal of achieving resolution or closure. The work that can be achieved here is more aligned with a softening of judgement and of expectation that any resolution is possible. Suicide by its very nature blocks resolution and requires those who remain to live with the questions and concerns it leaves behind. This experience can be acknowledged and shared and this, somehow, softens or releases something in the carrying of this most difficult of burdens.

Chapter 22

The Myth of Forgiveness

There is a great emphasis on forgiveness in many spiritual traditions and on its vital role in wisdom, compassion and authentic healing and closure. This notion has transcended the realm of the spiritual and has "gone mainstream" as an ideology that is now represented in a variety of literature and treatment and recovery programmes. It supposes that it is not truly possible for any individual to be free of suffering and unshackled from their past unless they have developed compassion for and forgiven those who they perceive to have injured them or done them harm. This principle has seeped into popular culture to the degree that many take it as a truism and hold it as an aim. As Robert Muller points out, "there is a culturally embedded expectation to forgive, and it comes at a heavy price, a sense of personal failing among those still haunted by their past" (Muller, 2018).

Forgiveness, however, is a problematic concept for survivors of abuse who endured such a sharp imbalance of power that was both deliberate and continuous. Yet it is often a hidden belief held by survivors that adds to the subtle sense that healing is impossible as forgiveness is too big of an ask. It is an important theme to draw out due to its often-hidden nature and its presumption of truth. Many survivors can feel damned due to their own rage and complete lack of compassion towards their perpetrators. It can be a valid further source of rage and frustration that they are somehow guided towards kindness and forgiveness of abusers as a worthy goal.

In her book *The Places That Scare You*, Pema Chodron, a renowned Buddhist nun, warns of the danger of "idiot compassion" which she describes as "When we avoid conflict and protect our good image by being kind when we should say a definite no" (Chodron, 2001, p.78). She points out that many people can use these ideals to justify self- debasement and perpetuate a habit of masochism and letting people walk all over us. There is a need to distinguish those people and situations where acceptance is not appropriate and to draw clear lines and boundaries.

It is not the forgiveness of perpetrators of abuse that is sought here. It is not useful or authentic to forgive those who have no remorse or regret and who remain abusive currently or deny the truth. The most common lack with regard to forgiveness is survivors' failure to extend forgiveness to themselves. In terms of healing and recovery, this is the forgiveness to seek. Forgiveness for having been hard on

DOI: 10.4324/9781003268888-27

The Myth of Forgiveness   87

themselves, for having blamed themselves for things that were beyond their control, for having judged themselves harshly or seen themselves as culpable when they were innocent. Forgiveness for having acted in ways that were not authentic due to a lack of choice, forgiveness for keeping the secret of what was happening however much it horrified them.

It is helpful also to examine the circumstances under which true forgiveness could be reached. In delving into this topic over the course of many groups the consistent factors which are essential for forgiveness to be authentic include:

1   Genuine remorse and regret on behalf of the perpetrator (words without real feeling behind them would be insufficient here and mere lip service would not suffice).
2   A clear and apparent cessation of all abusive behaviour.
3   Sincere attempts to make amends.
4   A willingness to hear and accept the victim's perspective.
5   Perpetrators presenting themselves to the authorities where appropriate.

It is important to note that all of this may still not result in feelings of forgiveness and that this is ok. As Pema Chodron notes, "forgiveness cannot be forced" (Chodron, 2001, p.82).

Questions for the Session

1   Do you believe that forgiveness is necessary in order to heal?
2   Do you encounter this belief in others?
3   How does it make you feel when this is said to you?
4   Under what circumstances can you authentically forgive?
5   Have you forgiven yourself?
6   What would make it possible to forgive yourself if you have not done so?

Example

Mavis is a 40-year-old woman whose father sexually abused her throughout her childhood. She told the group that a friend who had called around for coffee and had been aware of her history spoke to her about forgiving her father. This friend had an affiliation to a religious group that espoused forgiveness as an essential action in order to attain peace. Mavis spoke of how she had become enraged with this friend and was furious at the suggestion that this was necessary. It evoked a strong conversation amongst participants about the role of forgiveness in their own healing and revealed the worry for some that as they could not forgive, they would be eternally trapped in the past and never experience release from their suffering. This was discussed in the group and became a robust and healthy discussion on the role of forgiveness and the parameters in which it could be granted. As the group did not, on this occasion, identify the need for self-forgiveness, I brought this in as the therapist and intentionally directed the conversation towards this focus. The atmosphere changed significantly and the possibility of having heart for themselves opened up and was directly addressed in the space. This was experienced by all as deeply healing.

References

Chodron, P. (2001) *The Places That Scare You*. Boston, MA: Shambhala.
Muller, R. (2018) *Trauma and the Struggle to Open Up*. London and New York: Norton.

Chapter 23

The Question of Evil

For those who have experienced sexual, emotional and physical abuse or neglect, in a manner that was extreme, conscious, repetitive and deliberate and where the perpetrator displayed no remorse at any time, but rather registered enjoyment or pleasure, the question of whether this constitutes genuine evil will necessarily arise. It is an important question for survivors and deserves the therapist's attention and respect as a genuine enquiry. Despite its near theological territory and the fact that the therapist is not a theologian, nor purporting to be, it is well to give consideration to one's personal beliefs on the matter.

Once the client has worked through their past sufficiently to accept what has occurred to them as abuse, and no longer minimises their experiences, there is often a stage of questioning how someone could act in these ways and a search for mitigating circumstances or past abuses suffered by the perpetrator that might explain their thoughts or actions and lend understanding to the "why" of it all. This search typically concludes with the realisation that no difficult past experience, confusion of thought or morality or skewed projection is sufficient to provide an answer or a reason for such severe breaches of a child's trust and vulnerability.

Clients often correctly note that they have not offended in like ways despite their own abuse and that further, their total abhorrence to any like behaviour makes it clear that having been a victim of abuse in no way facilitates becoming an abuser. This is another problematic notion for many clients, who feel that they carry the seed of potentially being abusive due to the common narrative that most of those who offend have been abused themselves. Survivors can often police themselves mentally, in a harsh or rigorous fashion, waiting for rogue bad behaviour to emerge in a manner that they will have no control over. It has been the cause of many parents displaying less physical affection than they would have wished towards their children, in case it was somehow inappropriate. This is a myth that needs to be debunked in a very clear way.

Evil is variably defined as causing harm, pernicious behaviour, causing discomfort or repulsion or arising from actual bad character or conduct (Webster's, 2020). These definitions, whilst clear, do not go far enough and fall short of naming the mechanics of behaviour that is categorised as evil. Gabriele Amorth

DOI: 10.4324/9781003268888-28

90 Session Themes

describes evil as "the mistaken use of liberty, thus it has a personal foundation" (Amorth, 2019, p.35). The notion here is that evil action requires the will of the individual to engage with what is abstractly negative behaviour. A decision is required on behalf of the doer of evil to act thusly and the doer must experience some personal gain or pleasure in so doing. The wielding of power over another being is a characteristic of evil which must be twinned with a marked lack of empathy, as no discomfort is felt in seeing the discomfort of another. Psychopaths and sociopaths provide instructive languaging and understanding of "evil" traits and Bob Hare's Psychopath Test measures these features comprehensively and with clarity (Hare, 1975). M. Scott Peck's *The People of the Lie* is also an excellent illustration of behaviours that fall into this category and I would recommend it as valuable reading for those clients who are ready (Peck, 2006).

It is easier to locate "evil" in a perpetrator who comes from outside the family due to the lack of relatedness or any blood bond. When the abuser is a family member, particularly when they are a parent, this is a more difficult prospect. The idea of the good mother or father has a sacrosanct internal representation and is a hard one to overturn. It is usually felt as taboo to consider them bad people. It also raises the question of whether the client themselves is somehow inherently bad, as they are directly related by blood to the offender.

Questions for the Session

1   Do you believe that evil exists?
2   How would you define this?
3   Have you experienced or witnessed this?
4   How has this experience impacted on your view of the world?

Example

Stella spoke in the group about her mother. She said that she had been highly narcissistic throughout her childhood and continues to be so to this day. She colourfully described her mother's many devices to continually hold power and direct attention towards herself and away from anyone else, including her children. She said that these strategies ranged from aggression to creating feelings of guilt in others and portraying herself as a victim when this was not the case. Where Stella felt that her mother had been "evil" was in her physical brutality towards her and her siblings and in her knowledge that her children were being sexually abused whilst not acting to prevent this from occurring. She noted that her mother would actively send her and her siblings to overnight visits to a neighbour that she knew was abusing her children. Stella told how this had taken her a long time to acknowledge as it was so abhorrent to her that this could have been true of her own mother. She said that while it had been incredibly difficult to see her mother as having been evil, it had been liberating to name it and to "call a spade a spade". She said that it had helped her to see how unlike her mother she was and to distance herself in the present and maintain a very clear boundary without being pulled back in by guilt.

References

Amorth, G. (2019) *The Devil is Afraid of Me*. Nashua, NH: Sophia Institute Press.
Hare, R.D. and Cox, D.N. (1995) *Manual for the Psychopathy Checklist (PCL:SV)*. Toronto: MHS.
Peck, M.S. (2006) *The People of the Lie*. London: Cornerstone.
Webster's Dictionary (2021) "Evil". In *Webster's Third New International Dictionary*. Springfield, MI: Merriam Webster.

Chapter 24

Brokenness and Healing

There is a point when much work has been done, insights gained and change has occurred, when the question naturally arises as to how much healing is possible. Participants often reach a point where they express a feeling of irreversible contamination as a consequence of their abuse history and question the efficacy of any therapeutic endeavour to really rid them of the damage done. They question who they would have been if their experiences had been different and allow themselves to contemplate what they would have achieved had they not been so deeply traumatised.

This point is a very important one and marks a possible turning point in the understanding of one's essential self and one's being in the world. The desperation arises from the remaining parts of the person that feel rejecting of and angry at the pain they can still encounter. This aversion and judgement is completely understandable and needs to be tolerated and accepted. It is not unusual for the therapist to perhaps begin to feel a bit deskilled and unhelpful at this point and to catch a wave of overwhelm and hopelessness themselves. Rather than reject this place, the therapist needs to facilitate this conversation very openly.

It is poignant and evocative to ask participants who they imagine they might have been, what they think the picture and path of their lives would look like if they had had nurturance and support. This allows members to journey back to those parts of themselves that they liked and admired. There are often memories of great spirit, intelligence and ability that were not honoured or facilitated and a deep mourning for this potential child and her unlived life.

This journey back allows members to flesh out that being before others and to breathe life into her again. It is almost as though the child in question comes into the circle and impresses everyone, does a twirl or a bow, and walks out again. It permits participants to both reclaim those skills, characteristics and abilities for their present selves as well as grieving how much further they could have taken those elements had they been able.

This is one of those items that can bubble up at any time in the group process. It is often best looked at when it comes into the room spontaneously as this indicates that the group is well cooked enough to do this most valuable work. There is also value in debunking the myth that other children who did not have abuse in

DOI: 10.4324/9781003268888-29

their past automatically had an easy time of things or a life without struggle. There is room for acknowledgement that life contains many elements of struggle and an element of separating from the identity of being a victim of abuse can begin to budge. This was their struggle and trauma, and it is honoured and seen in the context of a world that is replete with a variety of struggles and traumas. It is also acknowledged that healing is not akin to having a lobotomy. Memories of the life we have lived will not simply disappear and leave us clean and unaffected, and this is not a realistic goal. There is often a significant relief in accepting this fact, particularly in the midst of a community that sees and understands the pain and yet has been able to find humour and companionship in their fellows.

Questions can go very deep at this time and reflect on the meaning of life and delve into a variety of personal beliefs. Participants often reflect on their faiths or lack thereof and how this informs their thinking and feeling.

Questions for the Session

1   Do you think it is possible to heal completely?
2   What blocks healing for you?
3   What gifts or talents or qualities did you have as a child that were overlooked or devalued?
4   How can you reclaim those?
5   Do you have a foundation of belief in your life, spiritual or otherwise, that helps you?

Example

Joe spoke passionately and with great frustration one session about the fact that he thought that no matter how much work he did or groups he joined, he was never going to feel completely better or really be free of abuse. The group was opened up to this topic, as it seemed pertinent due to the effect that Joes saying it had. There was a palpable sense of disappointment and frustration in the room as other group members agreed and felt that they were too fundamentally damaged to feel that they could ever heal. This was, in one way, slightly rude to the therapists who had been working hard in this milieu, it questioned what they were doing and if they knew what they were doing ... was there any point to all of this? The therapists then worked through the above questions with the group and questioned their expectations of healing. This allowed fantasy versions of what was possible to be discarded and a heartier acknowledgement of where the real value and efficacy was to be found in engaging in this process. Members spoke warmly of how they had affected and empowered one another and reflected how this sense of community and freedom to be authentic was, in many ways, as good as it gets.

Chapter 25

Inner Child Visualisation

This is a particularly strong and often beautiful session, or more likely pair of sessions. It is often a turning point in the work for many participants and it must be given the time to fully unfold and occur in an unhurried way.

The facilitators should introduce the session and give members a brief outline of the session at the conclusion of the preceding week. This has the advantage of summoning up the child inside and beginning to hold him or her in awareness. Members then have this child with them in a more fully fleshed out or vivid manner when they enter the session and can reap greater benefit from the chance to heal old wounded aspects. It can make the intervening week a more vulnerable and emotional place, which may be felt to be difficult, however the resulting healing should more than compensate for this.

The session commences with the inner child visualisation. This should take about 25 minutes duration and be well and thoughtfully guided. On conclusion of the visualisation participants are encouraged to move directly into the art piece without speaking. Members are simply asked to illustrate, in whatever of the available media they choose, to represent some aspect of their experience in the visualisation. They are asked to remain silent and to stay with themselves and their child throughout this exercise so as to not break the mood and healing that may be occurring. This should be given 20 minutes approximately, however it is preferable to monitor the group field and see how the time is moving and be led by that.

Participants are then asked to lay their work in a circle and to speak something about their art piece and their experience of the exercise. For some people, they capture their experience well in the art piece and for others this is not so but the work is a leaping off point to speak about how they found the exercise. It is always important to emphasise that this is not an art class and that there is no desire to produce anything visually impressive or even passable. The art is in the service of the experience and serves as a way into the conversation.

Questions for the Session

1   How did it feel to do this exercise?
2   Did anything surprise you?

DOI: 10.4324/9781003268888-30

Inner Child Visualisation   95

3   What have you captured or tried to capture in the art piece?
4   How do you feel sharing this?
5   Is there anything else you need to do following on from this experience?

Example

Most participants will recognise that the child whom they approach in the visu-alisation is themselves as a young person and respond accordingly. While the responses will vary they are typically characterised by a warmth and tenderness towards the child, with members either physically holding the child or speaking important words or messages to them. This exercise can bring home the reality of the young age they were when they encountered abuse or trauma and help to clarify the impossibility of them having held any responsibility for what occurred. One participant shared that she had painted herself holding the child's hand and noted that there had been a marked lack of physical contact or affection within her family. She recalled that the only physical attention she had received was abusive in nature and she shared that it had felt very healing to be able to offer the child an experience of touch that was caring and nurturing and that this was what she needed to bring more of into her life. She discussed the possibility of going for massages, which would have previously felt quite threatening for her. It was a healing encounter that allowed her to renegotiate an old story around the safety of touch and was profoundly moving to witness for all who were present.

Chapter 26

Endings and Beginnings

One of the central tenets of Buddhist philosophy states that change is constant. There is no way to be in life and not experience change and the joy or suffering that accompanies it. There is a deep understanding of the reality of impermanence and an encouragement to embrace and accept this truth as we are powerless to change it or affect it in any significant way. As Pema Chodron notes:

> The Buddha taught that there are three principal characteristics of human existence; impermanence, egolessness and suffering or dissatisfaction. According to the Buddha, the lives of all beings are marked by these three qualities. Recognizing these qualities to be real and true in our own experience, helps us to relax with things as they are.
>
> (Chodron, 2001, p. 17)

Truths, when laid bare like this, are hard to deny. We are unlikely to find anyone who states that nothing has ever changed in their life or experience. Transitions are essential; they are integral to the rhythm and flow of life and crucial to participating in the developmental process. To move from being a child to an adult involves countless physiological, psychological and emotional shifts. That the nature of change and impermanence is a natural thing may do little to soothe us in the face of unwanted or trying developments that can stretch us to the limits of our endurance or understanding.

It has been my own experience that it is common for a shift in perspective or a deep learning to be preceded by a period of stress, discomfort, confusion or chaos. Alchemically speaking, this is the "nigreda" (Jung, 1959). The struggle of understanding or wrestling within the self that lets die what needs to and makes way for a fresh insight or way of being or behaving in the world and in relationship, both with oneself and with others. This can be a hard passage and can be brought about by loss, rejection or any failure to maintain or achieve what was expected or hoped for. It is often true that we gain deeper understanding of ourselves, our blind spots and hidden aspects of our own nature through these experiences and this renders what is difficult meaningful and can be seen as a rich source of learning in retrospect. This is far more difficult to feel with endings and losses that are

DOI: 10.4324/9781003268888-31

Endings and Beginnings 97

traumatic. Trauma is typically characterised by a suddenness, a randomness and a lack of being in line with what is right, appropriate or timely. This is an ending that is abrupt, violent and hard – if not impossible – to reconcile oneself to.

For survivors of abuse, trust in the adult world, in justice and often trust in the family, is often the primary loss and it is indeed a traumatic one. This is a loss that occurs before there is any possibility to language or to negotiate it and it is felt as bewildering and shocking in every aspect, an end to innocence that cannot be restored. This early impact can render subsequent losses even more difficult to understand and manage than they would be ordinarily.

For many of us, whether we have experienced abuse or not, endings are not something that have been planned or approached with foresight but rather are something that has been foisted upon us unwillingly and from which we have had to understand and heal from on our own and at our leisure. Many of our experiences of endings are, in essence, experiences of loss. Death is the ultimate loss, but many of us have had little deaths of circumstance or relationship that may be poorly understood and unprocessed, leaving an internal fault line and sense of confusion. This confusion often results from a feeling that we have been misunderstood, judged or devalued in some way that we do not have recourse to fully address. We have been, we feel, abandoned and there is no forum in which to plead our case.

It is helpful in this session to explore the learning in the occurrence of endings and to identify the new beginnings that could not have been born without these losses. This helps to locate change and transition more usefully in the scheme of life and to question the need for fear and dread when negotiating change. It is also important to look at the impact of trauma on how endings are managed and the possibility that early trauma amplifies the fear felt at these nexus points.

The ending of the group is also an ending that is live and in sight. The 30 sessions will conclude and the close bonds that have resulted from sharing so openly and in safety will not have a meeting place in this format forever. It is helpful to ask how this group wishes to make their ending, to see what needs to be done and said prior to this looming event. This is put front and centre in order to allow members to make the most of the opportunity and have no regrets or loose ends when concluding. Despite initial wariness or even reluctance, it has been my experience that members gain a lot from having been able to speak honestly, and the 30 sessions go by swiftly. There is often an unspoken anxiety about ending and it is best to bring this out at the mid-point, so as to address any outstanding needs and to best position everyone to make a good and successful ending that has meaning and value.

Questions for the Session

1 How have you experienced loss in your life?
2 What was the most difficult aspect of this?
3 Does this continue to affect you?

4   Has someone ever lost you?
5   How could an ending be well managed?

Example

Jake spoke about a friend who "ghosted" him. He said that this had been a friend of many years and that he had never understood what had happened to end the friendship. Jake was encouraged by the group to revisit the story and as he reviewed what had happened in the group setting he gained new insight into what was likely to have occurred. Members asked Jake what the timing of the friendship breakup had been and if it had coincided with any changes in his life or the life of his friend. He noted that he had been very happy in his life at that period and had gained a promotion in work and met the woman who would go on to be his wife. Upon probing by the group members, Jake realised that his friend had been faring less well in his own circumstances and that he had not seemed happy for Jake's good fortune. The group members questioned whether this friend could have been jealous of his success and that this could have been why the friendship dissolved. Jake reflected more deeply in the group context that his friendship had flourished when they were both struggling and that when his own struggles ceased, so did his relationship with this friend. Jake said that it had never occurred to him that this could have been the case and he had always carried a sense of guilt or wrongdoing that he now felt was unfair. He noted that this had been a pattern he recognised from his family of origin. He came to see that his father and one of his siblings had not been supportive to him at moments of achievement but rather had perhaps been envious. He noted that this had led him to downplay his successes and feel guilty about achievements he was proud of. He became aware that he had feared not being accepted or liked if he shone too brightly and that this was no longer the way he wished to be. He thanked the group members for their (sometimes very robust) feedback and noted that he felt relieved of a burden that he had been carrying for a long time.

References

Chodron, P. (2001) *The Places that Scare You*. Boston, MA: Shambhala.
Jung, C.J. (1959) *Psychology and Alchemy*. London: Routledge.

Chapter 27

Ways Forward

To begin with, most potential group members balk at the thought of 30 sessions spreading out before them. The time involved seems long and unwieldy and often clients reflect that it seems a very big undertaking and most, even the more enthusiastic participants, enter the endeavour with some sense of ambivalence. This perspective changes once clients are in and engaged and morphs into a shock at the speed at which sessions are going by and a gnawing feeling that 30 sessions may not be enough. People who began as strangers have come to know and trust one another. The value that has been uncovered in experiencing a healthy peer community becomes a cherished thing and the realisation that this is transient and will conclude becomes palpable.

In acknowledging this truth we affirm the value of what is occurring and its impact on our life outside the group. This is an important bridging piece of work. It can be tempting to slightly languish in the belief that this group with these people is the only place where they can be met in truth and honesty. This is an understandable response and speaks to the difference in quality and depth of conversation and the personal visibility that members should be experiencing if the group is working well. It is too easy, however, to stay here. The work of the group therapists at this point is to help clients discern how they can adapt the learning and healthy communication that has unfolded into other contexts.

This notion can be met with some resistance initially with clients noting that others in their lives do not have the shared experience of abuse and therefore lack the ability to "get it" in the same way that fellow participants do. While this may be so at some level, it is important to lead the focus back to how this group formed their trust and style and to note the characteristics of risk taking, supporting and challenging that enabled this type of relationship to grow. These features are true of any mature and genuine relationship and clients can be encouraged to acknowledge the improvements that have been made in their own abilities here and in their ability to be able to recreate this in other spheres. Further endorsement that clients' powers of discernment have heightened through the group process can help to facilitate this belief in themselves. The group can reflect that it did not trust on sight but as a consequence of establishing a contract and felt sense of safety with one another based on increased risk taking and consistency of support.

DOI: 10.4324/9781003268888-32

This remains true for all other situations and is a knowing that has been embodied and can be carried forward with confidence.

It is important to identify in concrete ways those people, places and things that members wish to affect in their lives. Hidden or lost creativity may have been unearthed in some, relationship rifts that require addressing may be necessary, habits, situations or partnerships may require adjusting or conclusion, certain difficult conversations may need to be had. There is no prescription for the perfect life and that is not the aim; rather we seek to influence how we go forward armed with our newfound or deepened confidence and knowledge of the areas of our life we would like to apply our new learning. Some may need to take more risks or one significant risk in order to move things on in a way that feels healthy and growth oriented for them. Others may need to settle in to what they already have and to appreciate all that is there for them in a more profound way as they uncover gratitude about their lives, families and accomplishments.

Questions for the Session

1   What do you feel you have learned from taking part in this group?
2   Do you feel you have changed? If so, how?
3   What has surprised you? What did you not expect?
4   What did not change that you would have liked to be different?
5   What would you need in order for that to occur?

Example

Trevor had been an older child in a large family. His parents had been poor and he had been under pressure as a young man to earn money for the family and contribute to the survival of his siblings. He left school early and worked manually in order to provide this much-needed income. Trevor always felt that he had been denied his education and that he had potential that he had not reached due to lack of opportunity and his family's circumstances, which he acknowledged had been beyond anyone's control. He had always maintained an interest in visual art and photography in particular. At the close of the group, he applied for and was accepted to a well-known art college to study photography and he entered several competitions, which he gained ranking and profile from. He reflected that he would not have followed up on this prior to attending the group, but that the encouragement and compassion he felt in the group had enabled him to pursue his passion, finally, and that he had found a confidence and joy in embodying his creativity that he had not imagined possible.

Chapter 28

Closing Session

This session marks the culmination of a significant journey for all participants. It should be honouring of the work done and of any gains achieved. Participants will have been invited to consider how they would like to mark this juncture in previous sessions so that the idea has had time to percolate and a meaningful punctuation identified by each group member in a manner that is particular to them. There are no right or wrong or better or worse ways to do this. Length is no better or worse than brevity and a few well-chosen words are as valuable as a presentation with props. It is important that everyone is there and if there is a difficulty for anyone it is better to postpone than to press on for the sake of rigid scheduling.

Suggestions for Closing Ceremony

1   Bring in something that you feel describes the changes you have made or the person or qualities you have manifested through participating in the group.
2   Wear clothes that you feel celebrate and reflect you as you are today. (This can be more flamboyant than usual or even a fancy-dress costume! Fun and celebration are the main idea here.)
3   Bring a photo of yourself as a child or a favourite item, book or clothing that you have from that time to bring that lost child into the present or represent her on this day.
4   Bring a song/poem/story/dance that you like or have created to share.
5   Share something that you feel is a gift or talent of yours that the group may or may not know about.

Along with the individual pieces that participants bring, it is important to have a closing piece as a group. An art piece is particularly good at this point, as all members are familiar with the engagement with art as a process and it is not too heavy or serious. Lay out a large sheet of paper and provide a good selection of colourful paint and invite everyone to make their mark in some way on the sheet. The therapists may contribute to this if it feels appropriate, maybe after the group members have finished, in case it feels that it needs anything to tie

DOI: 10.4324/9781003268888-33

Session Themes

it together or that the therapist's presence is important to the group. The group members can all receive a printout of a photographed copy of the work and have this as a keepsake.

Example

One group's closing session went as follows. One member asked the therapist if they could play a song immediately following the relaxation. The song was "Just Like Fire" and echoed the themes we had been exploring in the work and brought through a strong sense of confidence and self-belief regardless of obstacles or judgements. Members were very moved and even tearful in a joyous sense and smiles and laughter erupted in the room. This was followed by another member making a most thoughtful and well-prepared presentation wherein they visually conveyed their journey through the counselling service and presented each member with a packet of flower seeds to plant to recall the special time they had spent together. Again all were very moved and touched by the gesture and the thoughtfulness. The next member handed out silk scarves to all participants and to the therapists; they had carefully placed supportive cards within the scarves that they had felt were appropriate to each individual. Other participants spoke graciously of the effect of having heard everyone's story and how this had positively impacted their self-belief and reduced their sense of being odd or different. One member said "I thought, if you guys are all so nice and ok, then I must be ok too". It is hard to convey the feeling in the room at these times, but there is a sense of depth, compassion, strength, understanding, worth and meaning and it is an honour to witness.

Appendices

Appendix 1

Visualisations and
Art Exercises

Anger Visualisation

Begin by taking deep breaths. Inhale through your nose until your lungs are full or almost full and then release the breath through the mouth naturally.

Do this five times and I will count these through with you.

It is not important to follow my exact timing but rather to use it as a guide.

Then return to the normal pattern of the breath. See if you can follow this without tightness or judgement but simply noticing your breath and its quality. Is your breath reaching into your belly, or heart or throat? Does it flow easily or have any catches or pauses? If you notice anything there is no need to judge it or to engage in any kind of story about it, simply notice it and move on.

Feel your body resting on the floor and allow yourself to sink as fully as you are able into the ground. Let all of your muscles melt with the warm relaxing feeling of just letting go.

More

Allow yourself permission to look closely at and to feel the emotion of anger. We do this knowing that there is nothing wrong with this feeling and that we wish only to know it better and help to make it our ally.

Know that you will not be overwhelmed and that your own system's innate knowing will not allow you to feel anything that you are not ready for.

Know that anything you do feel is your own wisdom wishing to be known and acknowledged and that there is no right or wrong to anything here.

When you are ready, recall a person or situation that resulted in the feeling or sensation of anger arising for you.

See if you can see how this was felt by you. Where in your body did you notice sensation? Did the sensation stay in one spot or move around? Was there a temperature to it? Is there an image that captures this feeling?

How do you feel you want to react when this occurs?

How do you actually react?

If these are not the same, where does your authentic reaction go?

106 Appendix 1

Can you remain with this difficult feeling or do you feel a desire to pull away from it?

Just notice it, like a scientist, with no judgement or story or engagement.

Then let this feeling leave your system. Give it permission to go and request that it show you what you need to know. Thank your anger for the gift of this knowing, and give it permission to move on with your blessing.

Return to your breath. Feel your body beneath you and know that the earth supports you fully. Let any remaining tension, heat or anxiety dissolve into the earth where it disappears harmlessly.

Become aware again of the room you are in and the space that you are sharing with others.

When you are ready open your eyes and stretch your body.

Safe Place Visualisation

Begin by sitting or lying in a comfortable position. It is best if your spine is straight and that your body is as symmetrical as it is comfortable to be. This allows the breath to flow freely and to bring optimum healing. If you feel uncomfortable at any time, just move as you need to adjust your position so that you feel well and at ease. Have a blanket to hand or place one over you as body temperature can cool when we are still for longer periods of time than is usual to us. You may wish to close your eyes or to hold them in soft focus.

Notice your breathing and rest the mind lightly on the breath, simply following the movement and rhythm of your breathing. It is natural for the mind to wander and this can be expected; when this happens, just return your attention gently back to the breath. Every time our thoughts gather and lead us along with them, we simply return to the breath as our anchor and we do so in an attitude of kindness and patience with ourselves.

Gently deepen the breath by taking a cycle of 20 slightly deeper breaths than your normal pattern. Do not force this in any way but gently extend your usual breath, breathing in through the nose and out through the mouth. Do not worry if you lose count of this, I will let you know when it is time to return to your natural pattern of breathing.

Let your breath come back to whatever is native to it today. Feel your body and the surface that it is resting against and notice the sensation of contact with the floor or the chair. Allow yourself to let go fully into the feeling of being held and feel confident that the earth is fully supporting you and will not let you fall. Allow any tension to dissolve in this feeling of being held and let the muscles relax and let go of their hold.

Imagine that you are in a safe place, the safest place you can envisage. This may be a setting in nature, such as a meadow of lush grass and sweet flowers, on a warm sandy beach by the sea, in a woodland glade with a lake, perhaps a snowscape with tall mountains and crisp white ground, or something else provided by the natural world that is special to you. You may feel that your safe place is indoors, in a special room that is either real or remembered or a place of your imagining, perhaps a cosy room with a log fire and soft chairs, a room filled with books or materials you can create with, maybe a big soft clean fresh bed, or a candlelit bath.

Know that you are completely protected here and that no one who is uninvited can intrude, this place is yours and will only ever admit things or people you choose.

Notice what calls to you and allow yourself to fully step into this place. See what sights and sounds there are. Is there any music or sounds of nature? How does this place make you feel? What are its scents? Are there any animals or creatures here with you? Notice the tastes and textures of this place and allow yourself to sit down and take rest here, absorbing the beauty and the qualities of all the elements present. Notice if you are alone or if there is anyone with you.

Notice if you want to get up and move around this environment or if you prefer to be still and allow yourself to do whatever feels natural. Take some time to be here and let the feelings and sensations sink in more and more deeply.

Know that this place is always here for you in your mind's eye and that you can always return to it if you feel in need of rest, support or retreat. Give yourself permission to return any time you wish to and feel that knowing or belief with confidence.

As you plan to leave this place for now, take another look around and breathe in all of the sense of benefit and wellness that you feel from being here. Know that that wellness remains within you and continues to nourish your body and mind for the rest of the day. Gently, in your own time, say goodbye to this place for now, knowing you can return.

When you feel ready, with your eyes still closed or in soft focus, return your awareness to your body resting on the floor or chair and note the contours of this surface against your body. Bring your attention back to the room and the space that you are sharing with others and, in your own time, stretch fully and open your eyes.

Healing the Child Within Visualisation

Begin by making yourself comfortable. It matters that you are warm, at ease and feel able to relax. If you notice any feeling of restriction of clothes, or feel too cold or warm at any time in this visualisation, you are always invited to have the freedom to move and do whatever is needed to provide yourself with comfort and wellbeing. You can sit or lie in whatever way you please and feels natural to you.

Once you are resting and comfortable begin by allowing yourself to settle fully in the room. Bring yourself fully into the present, allowing thoughts and plans to drift away. It is natural for thoughts and feelings to come and go, we do not try to push them away or to invite them, but simply notice them whenever they come and gently return to the breath. Thoughts can be seen as if they

108   Appendix 1

are a parade passing through – you look, you see and then you let them go by, unforced, unjudged.

Take note of your physical self. Lightly scan your body to see how you are feeling. Notice, without getting involved, any areas of pain, stress or tension. Notice any pleasant feelings, or neutral ones. Follow the natural pattern of your breathing and expand this by breathing in a slightly deeper way for ten breaths. Then return to the natural rhythm of the breath.

Begin this visualisation by imagining yourself walking on a country road. The sun is shining, it is warm but not too hot, a pleasant temperature. You can hear the birds singing and smell the scent of the warm grass mixed with the earth of the fields. There is a warm breeze, very soft and gentle, that brushes your face. The road stretches out before you and the air feels clear and nourishing. You continue walking, unhurried and at ease. There is nothing to achieve.

As you continue on your walk, you notice a field up ahead. This field has a particular beauty that draws your attention. There is a gentleness to the landscape and a sense of warmth and nurturance to this area that seems to call to you. You walk towards this field and notice that there is a large gate at the entrance. You reach out and lift the latch, which rises with ease for you, and push the gate out into the open field. As you walk in you feel the embrace of the land. There is a comfort, a holding that is hard to describe that feels welcoming; it is as if the land is happy to meet you. You feel as if somehow, you are home.

You walk in and take off your shoes. The grass is soft under your feet and tickles your toes in an enjoyable way. You may feel that you want to run through the grass or lie down and roll around or rest in it … allow yourself to do whatever feels right … you are free here to be exactly who you are.

As you look around and scan this landscape, you notice something in the distance, very small. It is difficult at first to make out but it seems that it is a person, a small person, a child. You begin to move towards them and you notice that they are playing happily, absorbed in their surroundings. They are so charming and childlike in their play that it is beautiful to watch, such freedom and innocence.

In time, they notice that you are there and look towards you with a feeling of warm welcome. They are happy to have you there and they come over to where you are and greet you. You see that this child is familiar to you, and you see that they know you and you them. You greet each other as old friends. You are happy and content in one another's company and you spend a few moments just playing along with their game and enjoying this time together. You notice details about them, their hair, their clothes and the mannerisms and ways that they are in themselves. You have strong feelings of love and care for them and at some point it feels right to speak directly to them. You tell them that they are very loved by you, that you know them and have never forgotten them, even though time has passed since you last were with them. You tell them that you know how things are for them, and that you have always known. You can see their good times and their bad. You let them know that all of their deep hurts and secrets and bad feelings are known to you and that you love them still and that you always will. You tell them that there was nothing they could have done to stop or prevent any of the bad things that happened to them and that they are in no way to blame. You are sorry that you were not able to help them in the past and that you were powerless to prevent their suffering. You tell them that you are not powerless now but that you have come here today to remove them from all suffering and difficulty. That you love them so dearly and can see how special and precious they are. That you will bring them with you to safety and love and wellness and that they do not have to be in fear any more. They are safe. They are reunited with you and you have everything you need to hold them in safety and trust and that they will now be free to thrive in the world.

The child looks at you with great love and relief, they are so glad to hear your words and they reach out their arms and wrap them around you in a warm embrace, telling you that they have been waiting for you. You remain in this nurturing embrace for a while, as long as feels right. When the time feels like it has come, you take the child's hand, who offers it freely, and you turn to walk from the meadow together. They are looking up at you smiling and there is a spring in their step. This child is with you now and will remain with you. She is an important part of you and of your world and is so happy to be restored to you. They leave the meadow with you and do not look back. You walk back down the road together, warmed by the sun and feel their small warm hand in yours and the delight at being together again, knowing you can never be separated. This knowing seeps into your bones and warms your heart. This knowing is now part of your own essence. You go forward from this place as healthy, restored, vital, loving and loved.

Allow yourself to feel again your body at rest, noticing gradually the sensations of the air against your skin and the floor against your back. Without rushing or opening your eyes, begin to recall the space that you are in, the room that you are sharing with others, all of whom have been on this journey with you. Notice how your body is feeling, notice how you are feeling in general. When you are ready, gently and lovingly return your awareness to the room and begin to slowly open your eyes and stretch yourself as needed. You have returned.

Appendix 2

Relaxations and Meditations

Progressive Muscle Relaxation

We gently enter this relaxation by sitting or lying comfortably. See that you are warm and in a position of ease that will be supportive and comfortable. It is helpful to have a blanket to cover yourself as your body temperature can lower during relaxations. It is best to lie or sit with your spine straight, as this allows the air to circulate more easily through your system, and for your body to be symmetrical. Do not feel that you have to be rigid; rather be relaxed but in a good posture.

We begin by nudging our attention to the present. We accept that we are here, now, in this location, and will be here for the next 90 minutes. We allow ourselves to be fully present, leaving aside, temporarily, any plans for the future or thoughts of the past. We consciously give ourselves permission to park any worries or concerns that may be with us, knowing that we cannot affect these for the next while and so we may as well let them go. In this way we can gain the most benefit from the following relaxation.

Notice your breath. This is done in a gentle manner without needing to force the breath in any way. How is your breath moving through your body? Does your breath flow freely, bringing nourishment to your physical self? Do you notice any areas of constriction? Simply notice what is there, without getting caught up in any stories about this, just witness it and let it go.

In order to deepen the relaxation we will take some deeper breaths. Begin by breathing in through the nose until the lungs are full or almost full, then hold this breath for a few seconds and then release the breath through the mouth with greater force, letting the breath just go, in a natural way.

Then just allow the breath to fall back into its own rhythm and rest the mind lightly on the breath. If thoughts and mental conversations arise, this is inevitable and does not need to be judged or reacted to; this is the mind's nature. When thoughts or feelings arise, simply observe them and let them pass by, like floats in a parade, not getting involved and not rejecting them. When you notice thoughts have arisen, softly return your attention to your breath and to the relaxation, without any negative self-talk for having wandered off.

Relaxations and Meditations   111

Bringing your attention to your whole body, as it is, in the here and now, sitting or lying down.

Simply let your mind rest on your physical form and notice, gently, without any judgement, how your body is feeling.

Scan your body from your head to your toes and notice any feelings or sensations that are there. You may notice the feeling of the ground or chair beneath you, the contact of your body with the floor, the sensation of clothing against the skin, feelings of hot or cold, sensations of pain or stiffness, pleasant sensations, or you may not notice much of anything in particular. There is no right or wrong to anything, we are simply noticing what is present.

Take your attention to your feet. Try to rest most of your attention there and feel into the toes on each foot, noticing any sensation you encounter, perhaps the feeling of fabric against your toes, or a sense of heat or cold, perhaps there is a numbness or a lack of any particular sensation. Whatever is there, we simply notice it. We move up slowly with our attention through the feet, noticing the arches of the feet and the tops of the feet as well as the heels and ankles. We gently move our awareness up through the lower legs, front and back, the shins and the calves, and move into the knees. We may be aware of tingling, joint pains, heat or cold in particular spots or we may feel whole fields or sweeps of sensation, or we may not feel much of anything; again, we are just noticing whatever is there.

We continue on through our upper legs, the thighs, front and back, large muscles that do a lot of work carrying us around, we notice if there is any tiredness or heaviness here, or any other feeling. We bring our attention on up through our hips and sitting bones, noticing whatever we feel at this level, these areas have the bones of the hips, the ovaries, the womb and the base of the spine, and we may feel many things all at once. Once again, just notice without judgement or getting caught up in stories, whatever is felt.

We then move our attention to the base of the spine, the tip of the coccyx, and will gradually travel up through the body at the level of the spine. We move up through the hips and into the sacral area, and the lower belly, noticing any sensation that arises.

From there we move up through the spine and the centre of the body, the area of the solar plexus. Notice how the centre of your body feels; does it feel like it has integrity or is it compromised in any way?

Move on through the spine to the area of the upper torso, the lungs and chest and see again how the breath is flowing through the lungs. Is your breathing easy? Is it deep or shallow? Does the breath reach down into the base of the lungs or use only part of them? Notice the heart and chest. Do you feel tightness or ease? Is there anything in this area that pulls your attention? Again, just notice this without creating further involvement and let it go.

Feel into your shoulders, often an area of tension and stress; the shoulders carry many feelings and emotions and are often impacted physically by this. What do you notice here? Do you hold your shoulders ready for battle or in

112   Appendix 2

defence? Do you have injury or tightness or pain? Is there a feeling of blankness or numbness?

Bring your awareness to your neck and throat. Do you feel any constriction or activity in this region? Any heat or cold or numbness?

Move on up through your jawline and the base of the skull, as if the whole head and face were brought into awareness. See how tight or loose the jawline is and notice if you are holding any tension here. Continue up the back of the head and into the skull and into the brain, noticing if anything is felt in this region.

Feel on up through the face, moving through the cheeks and the nose, up through the eyes and behind the eyeballs and into the temples and forehead.

Move gradually up to the top of the head to the fontanel, the very tip, the place that is soft in infants, and see if you can allow your attention to rest there for a moment.

Next, we will travel back down the body, but at a quicker pace. As we descend, we imagine that any tensions or discomforts that were noticed will be washed out or released. We imagine that the body is filled with water and that as we travel back down the body, this water level is dropping, as if a plug has been pulled in our feet and the water is draining out, taking with it anything that we do not need.

And so we move down through the head and face, the neck and throat, over the shoulders, down over the upper torso, the lungs and heart and chest area, over the solar plexus, the stomach and through the hips, down the thighs and the knees, passing over the lower legs, the shins and calves, and into the heels and the ankles and all along the foot.

Once again bring your attention to your toes. Do they feel any differently now than at the beginning of the relaxation? What has changed, if anything?

Become aware of your body as a whole again and see how it feels. Gently begin to bring your attention back to the room that you are in and are sharing with others. When you are ready, slowly open your eyes and stretch your limbs to bring yourself back.

Golden Light Visualisation

Begin by sitting or lying down in a position that is comfortable for you. Softly guide your attention towards your body and the physical sensations that are present. Notice the feeling of your body against the surface it is resting on and feel the pressure of the places where your body rests against the floor or the chair. Pay attention to the sensations on the surface of your body … the feeling of clothes against the skin, the feeling of hot or cold; perhaps this is the same temperature over your whole body or perhaps there are differences at different locations – just see if you can notice what is there.

Move your attention to your breath and follow the pattern of your breathing with the majority of your attention, allowing thoughts to come and go freely and naturally. Spend a few moments doing this. Deepen your breathing gently, as this

Relaxations and Meditations 113

allows you to relax in a deeper way and brings an ease to your system. Simply breathe in through the nose and out through the mouth in slightly deeper breaths and do this for a few moments.

As you allow your breath to gradually fall back into a pattern that is natural for you, imagine a golden ball of light resting at the top of your head. This is not solid but light filled and glows warmly and safely. This light is filled with the qualities of healing and compassion, these qualities are its very nature and essence. Very softly and gently, this light begins to enter your body at the top of your head and spread its light of healing and compassion. The light is warm in a pleasant way and as it spreads it brings a sense of relief from struggle and tension and a sense of kindness and nurturance that is noticeable. The light continues to move, gently and non-invasively, at a pace you are comfortable with, down through your entire head and face, calming and soothing as it travels.

The light flows gradually over your throat and neck and has a healing quality to ease and relieve any tension or tightness it encounters so that your system can be restored to balance. The warm golden light flows down over your shoulders and deep into the muscles and bones, bringing health, healing and release. You notice that your body is relaxing at a different level and that this light is steeping you in a feeling of loving kindness for yourself. The light moves on through the upper torso and touches the heart and the lungs; this area is filled with beautiful golden light and nourished by it, the heart takes whatever it needs from the golden light and is touched and eased by nourishing kindness. A softness takes hold of the heart and harshness and impatience dissolve. Allow yourself to feel this as deeply as you can.

The light continues to flow down through the trunk of the body and softly lights the centre of the body, filling the belly area and the solar plexus. All of the muscles and organs at this level can relax and let go, keeping nothing back from this healing light. The light travels to your hips and down through your back and lower back helping and healing all areas in need with its healing and loving light. Freedom and relief are felt by any areas of illness or difficulty, past or present, and there is a deep sense of being held in safety.

The light travels on through the rest of the body and moves gradually down through the legs flowing freely now throughout your whole system. Your entire body is filled with the golden light, which does not dim or fade, but rather brings the right amount of healing and love to wherever it is needed by you. This light travels freely and brings what is optimum for you, maybe you feel what that is or do not have any specific sense, either way, the light will do what is needed.

Feel your body as a whole and notice how it is to be filled with light. Allow this feeling of wellbeing and inner compassion and kindness to remain with you, knowing that it is right for you to be held in this feeling.

Gently bring your attention back to the sensation of resting against the floor or chair and notice again the points of pressure. Notice your breathing and thank your breath for bringing life and wellness. Become aware again of the space that is being shared and in your own time, gently return to the room and have a stretch and move around.

114   Appendix 2

Rainbow Meditation

Begin by finding a comfortable position, whether sitting or lying down. It is best to have your spine straight and your body symmetrical, so that how it is on one side is the same as on the other. Make sure that you are warm enough and comfortable enough for the next 30 minutes and have a blanket or warm sweater and soft pillow to keep cosy.

Bring your attention to your breathing. Be aware of the continuous cycle of breathing that constantly brings air and nourishment to our whole system and know that it does this without any need to attend to it. This is your life's breath and it is always available to you to help you to anchor, or focus, or be present. In order to deepen the breath we will breathe in through the nose and out through the mouth in a deeper way, breathing in until the lungs are full or almost full, holding the breath for a moment, and then releasing the breath through the mouth at a faster pace. We will do this five times and I will count these. Follow my count as close as is possible, knowing that it may not be exact but close.

Allow your breath to relax naturally back into its own pattern without adjusting this in any way. As you settle into the breath's rhythm, imagine a rainbow, clear and bright and shining with its different lights. The rainbow is clear and vivid even though it is only made of light and all of its colours sparkle with intensity and beauty.

Look first at the red light – see how it feels in you to absorb the colour red. Is there a feeling of heat or warmth? How does this red affect you? What red things does this colour conjure up? Fire, sun, cherries, tomatoes, perhaps something personal in this colour, a dress or item of clothing, a toy or piece of furniture or art? Do you imagine a scent that is red? Is there a feeling or emotion that is red? Allow the colour red to wash over you and notice how it affects you.

Notice next the vibrant orange colour. What sensations or feelings does orange conjure? Is this an energising colour or a calm one? Is there a scent of orange? Is there a mood or emotion? Think of orange things that you recall: fruit, sunsets, coral or more personal things that you associate with orange. Take a bath in the colour orange and see how it affects your mind, your body.

Then turn your attention to the colour yellow. Bright, light, shining yellow. Does this feel like a happy colour, or another feeling? Is there a temperature? A scent or perfume? Think of yellow in nature, buttercups, fruit, yellow rooms and images. Notice the effect of the colour yellow on your mood and on your body. Let yourself be dipped in yellow and notice how this feels.

Next look at the colour green. Rich vibrant and natural green. One of nature's most abundant shades, from deep dark green to light pale green, found in trees, grass, fields of green stretching for miles, meadows and woodlands. Do you notice any energy that fits the colour green? Any mood? Any scent? Cover yourself in the colour green and allow the feeling of green to immerse you and bring its benefit.

Bring your focus now to the colour blue. The blue of the seas and the skies, from clear blue cloudless skies and turquoise seas, to dark inky blues of the night sky and the midnight waters. Do you feel drawn to a particular shade of blue? How does this make you feel? In your mind? In your body and emotions? Is blue a calming or restful shade? Is it vivid or exciting? Blue in nature comes in the forms of flowers like bluebells, cornflowers, forget me nots. Does blue have a scent or perfume? An atmosphere? Dip yourself in the feeling of blue and notice how it feels.

Now see the deep violet colour. The rich purple blue shade that can be seen in iris flowers and beetroot and blueberries. There are so many shades of purple from deep aubergine to pale lavender. Which shade draws you to it? What is the quality of feeling or emotion? Is it calming or something else? What feelings does violet bring about for you? Is there a perfume of violet?

Feel that you have taken in the full benefit of the rainbow of colours and that these have given health and wellbeing. Notice if there is a particular colour that you feel you would like more of. Allow yourself to see and feel this colour, perhaps one of the rainbow colours or another colour.

Know that the colours are there to help and support us and that their healing properties are always available to us and that we can call on them at any time.

When you feel you have taken all that you need from the rainbow of colours, begin to bring your attention back to the room and to the shared space and gradually open your eyes and stretch your arms and legs.

Chakra Meditation

To begin, sit or lie comfortably in a position that feels comfortable. Make sure that your body is resting in a position that is easy for you to maintain, though if you need to move around or shift position at any time, just adjust yourself however you need to. From the place of sitting or lying still, begin to draw your awareness into your body. Pay attention, in a light way, to how your physical self is feeling at this time and be aware of any areas of tension or discomfort as you lie or sit. Perhaps there is no specific feeling but rather a general sense of your body with nothing drawing your attention. There is no right or wrong thing to feel.

Next focus on your breath and lightly follow the pattern of your breath. Breathe in for the count of five, hold for five and then exhale for the same count. Do this five times and then just let the breath fall back into its natural rhythm.

This visualisation works with the chakras, or energy centres, that appear as spheres of light, believed to be located along the body's central channel. These energy centres are thought to be vital aspects of our functioning and to inform our health and engagement with ourselves and in the world. This exercise aims to clear and free these energy centres from anything that may compromise their optimum functioning and help them and us to experience greater increments of health and wellbeing.

We begin by taking our attention to what is called the root chakra. This is located at the base of the trunk of the body in the area of the perineum. This chakra is associated with connection and belonging; it is related to our "earthiness" and our sense of being held and of having a place in the world. The colour of this chakra is red. Look at or sense this in your own system. Does it feel healthy and vibrant? Is it a vivid red or a dull shade? Do you feel connected to your body and to the earth? Do you feel loved and held within your own body? Feel that this circle of light brightens and spins and clears whatever it needs to have health and connection to the nourishment of the earth. Know that the earth is safe and holding. That the earth provides nourishment to you. Feel the health of that sense of belonging.

We move our attention up the trunk of the body to the sacral area, around the hips and the lower back, and we envision a ball of orange light. This light relates to how well we are with our own creativity. This is the reproductive place and the belly, where new life and new ideas originate. How well do we create? How well do you dream a vision for yourself and manifest it? Do you have gifts and talents within you? Do you express these gifts or hold them within? Notice if you have talents that are unexpressed and see if you would like them to be free. Feel that this circle of light becomes bright and clear within you.

Next we move to our solar plexus, the very centre of the body, and imagine a glowing yellow light circle. This is the place of personal power, of our own agency and will. See if you can feel into this area. Notice if you feel that you know what you want. This is a place of asserting what we desire, even just to ourselves, do you feel that you have taken your power in your life or does the will of others direct you? What would it take to claim this power? As you consider this, imagine that the yellow light grows clearer and brighter within you, bringing healing and strength to this area.

From here, we move to the area of the heart and chest. We imagine a circle of soft green light that radiates a loving glow. This is the area of feelings and emotions of love. Do you feel that you can give and receive love freely? Is it easier to give than to receive? How does the flow and ease of loving behaviour appear in your life? Do you notice any blocks or obstacles to fully embodying this aspect of yourself? How might these be freed? As we reflect on this we notice the soft green light glowing and clearing and removing blocks that impede us. This light restores ease and naturalness to the heart and the breath.

Next we travel up to the area of the throat. Here we imagine a circle of blue light that works to clear and free the throat. We reflect, do we speak freely? Are we able to say what we wish to say or are we choked by fear or other considerations? What would we like to say that we do not? What kinds of things do we dare not express? Do we express too much? As we look at this we see the blue light glowing brighter and clearing the area from anything we no longer need.

We move next to the area of the third eye, the centre of the forehead, and here we imagine a violet light, soft and glowing. This is the area of our intuition, our ability to know what is true and to hear and see what is unseen and unsaid. It is our own highest knowing that allows us to intuit what is true without having recourse to factual information. It is our instinct and our awareness.

Relaxations and Meditations   117

We ask ourselves do we trust our knowing and our instincts or do we override this sense? Do we question and doubt ourselves? As we reflect on this we see the violet light glowing and clearing and we feel a greater confidence in our ability to intuit what is true for us.

The final chakra is located at the tip of the head, the area of the fontanel in babies. Here we imagine a pure white light. This area relates to our connection to higher purpose, spirit, guidance or however we feel comfortable understanding grace. This may be a religious figure or belief but this is not necessarily so. We reflect on our relationship to this aspect of ourselves and notice if we feel connected to or supported by the diving, in whatever aspect. Notice if this feels positive or complicated and see the light clearing and becoming brighter as any blocks to connecting with your own aspects of grace are removed.

Notice how you are feeling as a whole following this. See how your system feels and if there is any area that you notice in particular. Just let your body rest and receive optimum health and blessing from the state of relaxation. When you are ready, make the intention to close these chakras or energy centres down, simply having the intention is enough. Notice again your body on the floor or in the chair and feel its contours against the surface. Wriggle your toes and fingers and stretch yourself fully. Gently open your eyes and return to the room.

Appendix 3

Assessment Form

1. What is motivating you to join this group at this time?

2. Do you have any previous experience of individual or group therapy?

3. What benefit did you derive from engaging in individual and/or group therapy?

4. What might you like to be different in this experience?

5. How do you typically position yourself in a group? (e.g. the leader, follower, joker, quiet one)

6. Would you like to position yourself differently?

7. Are there any factors hindering your full commitment to participating in this group? (e.g. education, family, work etc.)

Assessment Form 119

8. Have you any issues of active addiction?

9. Do you have a mental health diagnosis? Are you taking any prescription medication for this?

Appendix 4

Referral Form

Name of candidate

DOB

Address

Tel

How long have they attended individual therapy?

Brief synopsis of reasons for attending

On a scale of 0 to 5, with 0 being low and 5 being high, please rate the following:

Motivation level

Attendance rate

Level of trust and working alliance in individual therapy

Degree to which issues around their family of origin have been addressed

Level of personal isolation

Therapist's reasons for nominating this client for group

Therapist's name

Appendix 5

Confidentiality Contract

The group agrees to honour and respect the following in order to ensure the safety and confidentiality of all those attending group sessions.

We agree that anything that is mentioned or discussed in this group is to be kept confidential. This means that issues discussed within the group will not be discussed outside the group.

The only time the group facilitators are obliged to break this confidentiality is if they believe that a group member is in danger of hurting themselves or another person or if the group member discloses identifying information regarding childhood abuse. Facilitators are required, as mandated persons, to inform TUSLA of identifying information that is disclosed relating to the abuse of children that is either current or retrospective in nature.

Group members agree not to contact each other outside group times. The group will review this issue at the close of the group.

Group members agree that it is alright to acknowledge one another if they were to meet outside the group setting. However, if you are with another person when this happens, it is not permissible to give the other person's name or how you know them.

There will be no abuse of any kind towards one another. This means not physically intruding on someone's space and taking turns and being respectful when talking and listening to one another.

Each group member agrees not to make assumptions about other members and to behave in a non-judgemental manner in order to respect the integrity and individuality of each member.

In the event of a group member being deemed to have broken or transgressed the group contract, it is possible that member would be requested to leave the group. If this is necessary the group facilitators will meet with the member in question to explain why this decision has been reached and to find a suitable alternative to the group process.

All group members agree to commit themselves to attending regularly and to being on time.

In the event of a group member needing to leave the room, each member has agreed that they not leave the building before speaking to one of the facilitators of the group.

In the event of a group member deciding to terminate their contact with the group, each member has agreed that they will first speak to the group facilitator about this and then meet with the group for a final session where possible.

The group members agree to not take non-prescription drugs or alcohol prior to the sessions.

Signed _____

Date _____

Appendix 6

Invitation Letter

Dear _____,

We are writing to you about our group on Developing Self Confidence and Caring for Yourself. This group will be starting on _____ at _____. We are very pleased that you are able to join the group and we are delighted to welcome you and hope that it will be of benefit. In participating in a group like this we aim to grow in confidence and learn new ways to be kind and respectful to ourselves. We will do this through the use of relaxation sessions, artwork and conversation between the group therapists and participants. I am enclosing a leaflet for your information. We would be grateful if you could call _____ to confirm your attendance.

It can take courage to risk doing something new like this and we are grateful for your bravery! We believe and have experienced that the benefits of coming and taking part will well outweigh any initial nervousness. We really look forward to seeing you.

Yours sincerely,

Appendix 7

Information Leaflet

How Can I Be Sure That It Is Confidential?

At the first meeting of the group it will be important to establish ground rules about confidentiality, respectful behaviour and boundaries.

As you are sharing personal information within this group, it is important that you feel safe to do so. This will be the case for all those participating.

The group facilitators and the members of the group will establish a *Group Contract* during the first session. This contract will be designed to facilitate confidentiality and safety for all group members.

Considerations

Group members are expected to attend weekly and adhere to the group rules. Each member must take personal responsibility to be present and on time for all meetings for the group to run effectively.

There may be times when you do not want to attend the group. It is during these periods that you are particularly encouraged to use the group to work through issues.

In cases of emergency, where it is not possible to attend, we would ask you to contact one of the group facilitators as soon as possible.

Details of Group

For details of all groups currently running in the service please ask your counsellor

Location:

Date:

Day:

Time:

Facilitators:

For any further information please contact:

Counselling Service

For Adults Who Have Experienced Childhood Abuse

Therapy Group

Information Leaflet for Clients

Introduction

Have you ever thought about joining a group or wondered what it would be like?

This leaflet gives you information about what group therapy is and answers questions commonly asked by people.

What is Group Therapy?

Group therapy is therapy that occurs within a group setting. Many clients progress to group work as a further stage of their therapeutic journey. It is a process where issues can be explored with others in such a way as to enhance your understanding of the effects of abuse on your life. It can provide a safe community in which to honestly explore subjects and feelings that many find difficult to address.

Thinking about Joining a Group?

In considering joining a therapy group, you may have many questions, concerns and anxieties. These may include meeting new people, perhaps recognising or being recognised by another participant and fear of revealing aspects/information about yourself to others.

What will I be expected to talk about?
Will I have to tell them about myself?
Maybe my abuse is not bad enough?
It's too awful to say what has happened to me.
How can I trust them?

All of these responses are perfectly normal and understandable. Remember that all participants are in the same position as you and are likely to have similar concerns and questions.

How Might Group Therapy Help Me?

Group therapy allows the survivor of childhood abuse to work through the effects of their abuse with others experiencing similar difficulties. Particularly a feeling of isolation and of "being the only one" is frequently experienced by survivors.

Group allows for each member to explore feelings, thoughts and beliefs that are no longer of benefit in their lives within an empathic and supportive space.

How Do I Join?

Discuss group with your counsellor. He/she will assist you in the process of going toward group work.

Who Will Facilitate the Group?

The group facilitators are therapists working in the service who have experience of group work. The facilitator/s will provide an environment that will enable each member to achieve personal benefit from their participation in the group. This means facilitating members exploring issues in a confidential, safe and supportive setting.

Being in the Group

How Often Do I Have to Attend?

Group sessions are held on a weekly basis at a regular time slot. There are 30 themed sessions with an option for a further ten less structured sessions.

Who Will Be in the Group?

The group will consist of no more than eight members who have experienced childhood trauma and two facilitators.

What Will We Talk about in Group?

In this group the facilitators will present and help the participants explore the places and subjects where we may be caught or have experienced difficulty; issues of trust, parenting, self-esteem, assertiveness, anger management, difficulties with intimacy, relationships and sexuality. The group will use relaxation exercises to open each session and art and visualisation exercises to aid exploration and understanding.

What Do I Do in Group?

In group therapy it is important to focus on the here and now, to become aware of your own feelings and thoughts and to learn to listen to self and others and move on from the past.

You have a unique and valuable contribution to make to the group and your commitment and participation can enhance what you can gain from this experience.

Appendix 8

Eligibility Criteria

1   Punctual and regular attendance.
2   A minimum of nine months to one year individual therapy. (This may be negotiable in some cases, discuss with group therapist if this arises.)
3   The client's abuse has been addressed and worked with in therapy to the extent that no significant idealisation of the perpetrator exists.
4   Family dynamics are in the client's awareness to some extent.
5   A piece of transference work has occurred within the individual therapy and been successfully resolved.
6   No active addictions to non-prescription medication or alcohol.
7   A willingness to commit to attending the group for its duration.
8   Client must not have narcissistic personality or borderline presentations.

Note: When speaking to your client about their possible involvement in a therapeutic group, please ensure that they know it is based upon assessment and evaluation. It is important that it is made explicit to clients that their admission or non-admission may be due to factors of suitability or practicality and that it in no way reflects on them in any negative manner.

Appendix 9

Note-Keeping Template

- What are the emerging themes in today's session?
- What sub-groups formed in the session?
- How do these sub-groupings relate to the family of origin?
- What roles were the therapists occupying in the session?
- Was any group member excluded?
- Was any group member silent?
- If any distress occurred, how was this handled or tolerated by the group?
- Did the therapists experience any difficulty or strong reaction to any member, including one another?

Appendix 10

Feedback Form

1. What were your hopes and expectations of the group?

2. Were these hopes and expectations met? If so, how? If not, why do you think this was?

3. To what extent did participation in this group help you to learn to recognise your personal, emotional and physical needs?

4. Since being in the group what do you think has changed most in the ways that you:
    a. Think
    b. Feel
    c. Behave
    d. Relate.

130 Appendix 10

5. What did you personally find the most helpful? Can you say why?

6. What did you find the least helpful? Can you say why?

7. What were the most important challenges you personally faced in the group?

8. What do you feel you gained from those challenges?

9. Were there any challenges you did not choose to face?

10 How were the group facilitators?
   a. Most helpful
   b. Least helpful.

11. What could be done differently to help this experience be improved?

Index

abandonment and controlling behavior 67
abuse 75; survivors 66
actively traumatised clients, as criteria for exclusion 9
addictions, as criteria for exclusion 8–9
Amorth, Gabriele 89
anger 66–68, 76; access 70; identification with 67; principal 66; visualization 67, 105–106
Art Therapy for Groups 45
Assagioli R. 5, 5
assessment for eligibility 10–14; colleague as referring agent 12; conduct of 12–14; eligibility criteria 13–14; referring own client 11–12; time of 13
assessment form 118–119
aversion and judgement 92
avoidant techniques 81

"badness" 66, 75
Benson, J.F. 8, 28, 30, 57
boundaries, in therapeutic work 44–45; emotional 50–51; physical 49–50
brokenness and healing 92
Buddhist philosophy 96

candle visualisation, 80
Casement, P. 29
chakra meditation 115–117
Change: Principles of Problem Formation and Problem Resolution (Watzlavik, Weakland and Fisch) 30
check in, in therapeutic work 37–38
check out, in therapeutic work 39–40, 46
children in abusive families: as golden child 61; as protector of sibling or siblings 61; position of being blamed 60–61; role as parent/caregiver 60

child visualization 94
Chodron, Pema 36, 86–87, 96
closing ceremony 101
concept for survivors of abuse 86
conceptual frame of reference 72
confidentiality contract 121–122
confusion 97; discordant feelings 64
co-therapist 27, 29
counterintuitive process 80

depression 70
"dirtiness" 74
disappointment and frustration 93

Eco, Umberto 67
eligibility criteria 127; accomplishment of one-to-one work 7–8; attendance and punctuality 6–7; commonality of experience 6; motivation and clarity of purpose 8; safety 6; sense of solidarity 6; trust and consistency 7
emotional: abuse 74; boundaries 50–51
emotion of anger 67
Erickson, E. 75
Estes, Clarissa Pinkola 69
"evil" 89–90

familiarity 83
family, encountered 57; extended 58; in macrocosm/societal context 61–62; parents 58–59; siblings 59–60
fear 80–82; based reaction 81
feedback 22, 46; form 12–130
feelings of abandonment 84
feelings of loneliness 70
Fire 67
forgiveness 86
formal processes 65

132 Index

Golden Light Visualisation 112–113
granting permission 67
grief and depression 69–71; healing 70; meaning 69; overview 69; undesirability of reaching 70
grooming: methods 76; process 74–76
group 99; cohesiveness 6; members 83; process 38–39; recording 23; referral 8, 10; treatment for childhood abuse survivors 1

Hare, R.D. 90
Hawkins, P. 30
humour, usage in sessions 47, 55

"idiot compassion" 86
impact of trauma 97
information leaflet 124
intimacy, in relationship 11, 18, 20–21, 30, 52–53, 60
introductory session. *see also* therapeutic work: art work 45; check out 46; discussion about safe place 45–46; by lead therapist 43–44; rules of confidentiality and guidelines for boundaries 44–45; safe place visualization 45; styles of communication 44
Inventing the Enemy 67
invitation letter 123

"Just Like Fire" (song) 102

lead therapist 28
Lew, M.: impact of being a "victim" 15; *Victims No Longer* 15
Liebman, M. 45

measurement of success 22
meditation: chakra 115–117; rainbow 114–115; visualization 19, 21, 35–37
members 64, 84, 93–94, 98, 102
mini group 27
mixed gender group 15–17; establishing pathways and understandings 17; positive mothering and fathering 16; preparations 16; promoting conversations outside of room 16; roles of clients 16–17
Mollon, P. 74–75

Muller, Robert 86
myth of forgiveness 86

narcissistic clients, as criteria for exclusion 9
nigreda 30
note keeping 23; template 128
"nurturance" 75

one-to-one therapy 11
open conversation 78

Page, S. 30
participants 93–94, 102
patterns and reactions 67
Peck, M.S. 90
perpetrators 75–76; of abuse 10, 86; as criteria for exclusion 10
personality disorders, as criteria for exclusion 9
"perversion" 74
physical: attention 95; boundaries 49–50; and sexual issues 78; violence 66, 74
piece of art therapy 68
Pinkola, Clarissa 69
principal anger 66
progressive muscle relaxation 110–112
psychological and emotional shifts 96
Psychopath Test 90

qualitative measures 22
questions for session 48

rage 66–68, 77
rainbow meditation 114–115
referral form 120
referral process: colleague as referring agent 12; referring own client 11–12
relaxations and meditations 110
Rinpoche, A. (Lama) 36–37
root chakra 115

"safe" 73
safe place visualisation 45, 106
safety-based visualisation 80
self-assertion 54–56, 81
self-awareness 47
self-blame 64
self-knowledge 47
self-worth 54–55

sensuality and sexuality 78–79
session 94, 101–102
session structure. *see* therapeutic work
sexual: abuse 74; desire 79; emotional and
    physical abuse 89; life 79; world, 78
shame 74
Shohet, R. 30
skewed projection 89
speaking out or standing up for oneself or
    others 54–56
Start Where You Are 36
suicidal ideation 83
suicidality: topic 83
suicides 83, 85
supervision 27, 29–31; internal, 29;
    models, 30; skilled therapist and, 31
supportive cards 102
supportive group framework 78
survivors 83, 89; of abuse 97

The People of the Lie 90
The Places That Scare You 86
therapeutic group. *see also* virtual groups:
    appropriate number 5–6; choosing
    members 5; criteria for eligibility (*see*
    eligibility criteria in group process);
    criteria for exclusion (*see* unsuitable
    candidate); mixed gender group, 15–17;
    practice of "right relations" 5; trust
    among members 5
therapeutic relationship 11; with co-
    therapist 29; with lead therapist 28;
    supervision 29–31
therapeutic work 27–28. *see also*
    introductory session; check in 37–38;
    check out 39–40; choosing a colleague
    to co-work 27–28; flexibility and
    accommodation in 38, 40; group
    environment 40; group process 38–39;
    meditation/visualization 35–37; order
    of sessions 40; questions for session 48;
    time frame 35
thoughts 107

time frame of therapeutic work 35
transference and counter transference 23
transitions 96
trauma 97
Trungpa, Chogyam 69
trust, in relationship 7–8, 16–17, 21, 30,
    39–40, 52–53
tyrants 62–64; dynamics 64

unproductive state of loneliness 72
unpunctuality, as criteria for exclusion 10
unsuitable candidate 8–10, 13; actively
    traumatised clients 9; clients with
    addiction issues 8–9; clients with
    personality disorders 9; narcissistic
    clients 10; perpetrators of abuse 10;
    unpunctuality 10

verbal responses 81
violence and emotional abuse 74
virtual groups: challenges 19–21;
    emotional space 21; mediation effect 21;
    privacy of members 19; technological
    glitches 20; teleconference modalities
    18
visualization 67, 95, 115; anger 105–106;
    art exercises 105; candle 80; golden
    light 112–113; healing the child
    107–109; safe place 106
volatile partners 81
vulnerability: domino effect 83

web-based meeting platforms 18. *see also*
    virtual groups
we-ness value 6
Women Who Run with the Wolves 69
working in a group 16–17
Working More Creatively with Groups 39
workplace harassment 64
Wosket, V. 30
"wrongness" 66

Yalom, I.D. 6

Printed in the United States
by Baker & Taylor Publisher Services